The Military Life of

WINSTON CHURCHILL
OF BRITAIN

Winston S. Churchill at age seventy-six. (UPI)

The Military Life of

WINSTON CHURCHILL

OF BRITAIN

by TREVOR NEVITT DUPUY
Col., U.S. Army, Ret.

FRANKLIN WATTS, INC.

575 Lexington Avenue
New York, New York 10022

This book is dedicated to
BILLIE P. DAVIS

SBN 531–01881–4
Copyright © 1970 by Franklin Watts, Inc.
Library of Congress Catalog Card Number: 69-17459
Printed in the United States of America

1 2 3 4 5 6 7

Contents

Foreword

There is general agreement among historians, as well as among a majority of the middle-aged general public, that Winston Churchill was the greatest man of our times, and one of the greatest Britons of history. Yet many military historians accord this honor reluctantly, attributing to him many mistakes and misjudgments in the field of strategy and of military affairs in general. They assign to him the responsibility for the failure of the Dardanelles-Gallipoli operations in 1915 and for the failure of the Norwegian operations in the spring of 1940; they criticize as naïve and shortsighted: his strategical views regarding the "soft under-belly" of Europe later in World War II, his stubborn efforts to thwart American plans for the Normandy invasion in 1943 and 1944, and his constant and reckless meddling in military details that he did not understand throughout the war. It is his inspired personal leadership of the British people throughout World War II, and the magnificent oratory which epitomized this inspirational capability, which these critics will admit warrant the accolade of greatness.

It has long been my view that Churchill was right in his

concept of the Dardanelles and Gallipoli operations, and that he was right in his assessment of the long- and short-range strategic significance of operations in the Balkans and the Danube Valley in World War II. I tended to be generally sympathetic to his views in other strategical and operational aspects of World War II, and felt that Sir Arthur Bryant was far too critical in his editing and commentary on the Alanbrooke memoirs, *The Turn of the Tide* and *Triumph in the West*. But until undertaking the research for this book, I was never absolutely certain that I had not been blinded to the realities of Churchill's shortcomings by the charisma of this remarkable man.

Now, at long last, having the opportunity to write a military biography of Churchill, my earlier views are not only confirmed, but reinforced. For reasons which I hope are adequately presented in the Introduction, I not only consider Churchill to be one of the most towering figures of world history, but in an essentially military sense I have—to my own astonishment—come to the conclusion that he demonstrated an ability as a strategist and as a director of war that merits including him in the select company of the great captains of history.

The principal sources for this book have been three of the major writings of Churchill himself—*The World Crisis* (including the two later volumes added to the work), *The Second World War*, and *A History of the English-Speaking Peoples*. As with Julius Caesar, whether or not one admires Churchill, it is impossible to assess his role in history without reference to his writings. I have given full consideration to views presented in more critical works, such as those of Arthur Bryant, cited above, those of Trumbull Higgins in *Winston Churchill and the*

Dardanelles and *Winston Churchill and the Second Front*, and *The Memoirs of Captain Liddell Hart*. In comparing with these rebuttals Churchill's own unquestionably biased presentations of his actions in controversial affairs, it is interesting to note how selective Higgins, Liddell Hart, and others are in their quotations from Churchill and from his enemies, sometimes presenting such quotations out of context, whereas Churchill invariably includes full texts, and much that is unfavorable to his various causes, as well as (understandably) everything that is favorable.

Other sources referred to include my own multivolume Military Histories of World War I and World War II, *The Encyclopedia of Military History* (in collaboration with my father), and other sources mentioned for earlier volumes in this series on the Military Lives of Hindenburg and Ludendorff and of Adolf Hitler. Among the biographical sources were Virginia Cowles's *Winston Churchill, Churchill from the Diaries of Lord Moran*, the Illustrated London News' *Winston Churchill, The Greatest Figure of Our Time*, Paris Match's *Hommage a un Géant: Churchill*, and the two volumes of Randolph S. Churchill's *Winston S. Churchill* that had appeared when this was written.

I have been greatly assisted in the research for, and writing of, this book by my colleague, Grace P. Hayes, who shares my admiration of Churchill. It is a pleasure to acknowledge the importance of her contribution to whatever merit this book may possess. But in the last analysis, the writing is mine, and the responsibility for errors and misjudgments is mine alone.

T. N. DUPUY

xi

Introduction

Winston Churchill had three careers. He started as a military man. While still a soldier on active duty he began to write serious, interpretive military history, and by the end of his life was known as one of the great writers of history of his time. He was still a very young man when he became a politician, which was to be his principal calling for the next fifty-five years. But during those years he continued to be a serious student of things military and played a leading role in the military affairs of his nation in peace and war. While he was making history—in a way and to a degree unmatched in his times—he continued to write his incomparable histories.

In this book we are only indirectly concerned with the fact that Churchill was probably the greatest politician, and perhaps the greatest historian, of his time. We are interested in his military career.

Winston Churchill was a very controversial man—most great men are. But in his case, it is possible that no other man in history—not even Alcibiades or Julius Caesar—has been so continuously involved in major controversy. Many will challenge

xiii

an assessment that suggests that he was the greatest strategist and war director of his time. Yet I will go farther. I believe that the pages of this book—which condense an exceptionally long and active career—will show that Churchill's genius in military affairs was so great as to warrant his inclusion in that select group of military leaders from the pages of history commonly called the Great Captains.*

Churchill first clearly demonstrated his natural potential genius for military leadership** in 1911. Although he had resigned from active military service more than twelve years before, when only a junior lieutenant, his study of military matters in general, and of the European strategical situation in particular, prompted him to make a presumptuous written assessment of the highly secret German war plan. He was at that time the British Home Minister, with no military staff or advisers to help him in this assessment. Yet he succeeded in doing something that had defied the General Staffs of France and Britain: He correctly analyzed the essential nature of the German secret concept for war known to history as the Schlieffen Plan, even to the extent of predicting the exact time—40 days after German mobilization—when an Allied counterattack might be successful. Three years later, in 1914, the Battle of the Marne ended in German defeat 41 days after mobilization.

---

* This group includes the following seven military leaders: Alexander the Great, Hannibal, Julius Caesar, Genghis Khan, Gustavus Adolphus, Frederick the Great, and Napoleon.

** See Appendix for a discussion of the characteristics of military leadership, and for a discussion of the nature of strategy, tactics, and military principles.

But in 1911 professional soldiers scoffed at this amazingly accurate forecast.

Historians today are prone to think of Churchill as a man who demonstrated flamboyance by playing hide-and-seek with the Boers; who as a young politician played cops and robbers in the streets of London; who rushed dramatically to Antwerp at the head of a naval brigade in September, 1914, when people thought he should have been at his desk in London; who perhaps foolishly tried to keep Edward VIII on the throne during the pre-abdication crisis; and who united Britain in World War II by speeches about "blood, toil, tears, and sweat." This true, but distorted, picture obscures the equally true image of the Churchill who was not only a student of military affairs, but also the first to introduce the concept now called "operations research" into the analysis and solution of military problems.

It was this scholarly, analytical, yet at the same time imaginative, Churchill who realistically prepared the Royal Navy for its role in World War I, and who overrode naval professional advice in instituting the strategy of distant blockade of Germany, the single most important determinant of Allied victory in World War I. He was also the first person on either side in World War I to really understand the nature of the trench stalemate on the Western Front. The measure of Churchill's genius is the fact that as early as October of 1914, he was developing concepts which caused him to be more responsible than any other man for the creation of the modern tank.

After World War I, Churchill was the first to review and analyze the casualties of the opposing sides on the Western

Front. This was a thoroughly documented evaluation of lasting validity, with conclusions that have only been confirmed by later studies of teams of specialists.

Churchill was the first man to assess—quantitatively as well as qualitatively—the implications of the rearmament of Germany under Hitler. A lonely politician, shunned by both major political parties, in 1934 and 1935 in the House of Commons he publicly made predictions of the comparative trends of declining British and growing German air-force strengths which were vehemently denied and scorned by the Prime Minister and the Air Ministry. Yet in early 1936 the Prime Minister had to make a public acknowledgment that he and the entire British government had been wrong—Winston Churchill alone had been right.

Churchill's imaginative genius came up with a multitude of new, and frequently successful, ideas on tactics and techniques during World War II. One of these ideas, which he produced during World War I and revived while Britain was under German air siege in 1940, was the production of artificial harbors to be used by British troops for an invasion of Hitler's Europe. It was at this time also, incidentally, when most of the world was expecting Britain to be overwhelmed at any time by a German invasion, that this man of genius calmly ordered Britain's only ready armored force to be transferred from England to Egypt. He knew that this force could not play a significant role if the Germans landed in Britain (which he did not expect); it could and did play an important role in crushing the Italian threat to Egypt and the Suez Canal.

Churchill was the first man of importance after World War II to comment publicly—and responsibly—on the significance and interrelationship of the two greatest military facts of our times: nuclear weapons and the cold war. He first visualized the realities of modern nuclear deterrence, when he spoke of the possibility of "peace [as] the sturdy child of terror."

Yet what of the criticisms that Churchill was responsible for the disastrous British Dardanelles and Gallipoli operations in World War I? And that he was unrealistic and naïve in his strategic concepts in World War II, particularly with respect to his obsession with the Mediterranean and the "soft underbelly" of the Axis?

As to the first of these, the record is clear. Churchill's original concept was for a joint army-navy assault on the Straits; an operation which even his most severe critics have admitted would probably have been successful. The idea for an entirely naval assault on the Straits was first proposed by the admiral who later most violently attacked the concept. Churchill adopted the idea only because the army refused to participate. Yet if his subsequent plan for this operation had been carried through with the determination he expected, it probably would have succeeded. When the army assault finally did take place, Churchill was horrified and disgusted to discover that there was no simultaneous naval attack. The failures at the Dardanelles and Gallipoli were not due to mistakes in strategic concept; they were due to failures by others, over whom Churchill had no control.

The second of these criticisms is less easy to refute. We do not know what might have happened if there had been extensive operations either in the Balkans, or in the Danube Valley, or both. It is hard to see, however, how the combined military might of America and Britain—which could succeed in a Normandy invasion, which could build a Ledo Road, and which could support armies or navies anywhere on earth—could not have coped successfully with the problems of operating in the Balkans and on the fringes of the Alps. Churchill's interest in such operations resulted from his realization that in World War II, as in 1914–18, it was vital to plan not only how best to defeat the enemy, but also how to defeat him and end the war at places and under circumstances most important for the peace that was to follow.

Those who accuse Churchill of wishing to avoid a direct confrontation with Germany in northwest Europe are wrong. Even while the British armies were being evacuated from Dunkirk, Churchill was already thinking of how and when and where he could return them to the Continent to wrest the final victory from Hitler. He desired and was committed wholeheartedly to the Normandy landing. But he did not permit this determination to become an obsession that would prevent him from seeing how the superior sea power of Britain and the United States could best be employed to support that climactic operation, and to assure that it would be successful with the least possible cost in precious manpower.

Churchill's was a farsighted, imaginative, strategic concept, worthy, in my opinion, of the most brilliant strategic intellect since Napoleon, and the most brilliant political intellect since Bismarck.

xviii

The Military Life of

WINSTON CHURCHILL

OF BRITAIN

Winston Churchill, age twelve, as a schoolboy at Harrow. (UPI)

Churchill as a cadet at the British Military Academy at Sandhurst. (UPI)

CHAPTER 1

The Young Soldier

Winston Churchill was born on November 30, 1874, in Blenheim Palace in Oxfordshire, England. The palace was named after the place where his illustrious ancestor, John Churchill, the Duke of Marlborough, won his most renowned victory. Winston's father was Lord Randolph Churchill; his mother had been Jennie Jerome of New York. Winston was thus half-American by ancestry.

The youthful Churchill did not do well in school, and he himself later wrote that his father had "come to the conclusion that I was not clever enough to go on to the bar." He twice failed the entrance examination into the British Military Academy at Sandhurst. But he finally passed and graduated from there eighth in a class of one hundred and fifty. He became a subaltern, or second lieutenant, in the 4th Queen's Own Hussars in 1894.

The ambitious young subaltern was bored by his first year of garrison life in England. So, when he had two months of leave in 1895, he obtained permission to go to Cuba as an observer with the Spanish army, then engaged in fighting a nasty little guerrilla war against revolutionaries, a conflict which three years later grew into the Spanish-American War. While accompanying Spanish forces in Cuba, Churchill came under fire several times.

Before leaving London, Churchill had thoughtfully arranged with a London newspaper to write a series of articles about the fighting in Cuba. So it was that in this, the very first war in which young Winston Churchill was engaged, his experiences were published. He began to think of himself not only as a soldier but as a writer as well.

The following year Churchill's regiment was ordered to Bangalore, in southern India. He stayed in India for two years. As an officer, he was involved every morning in drill and training, but in the afternoons he played polo. For hours each day he also devoted himself to an intense program of self-education, reading history, philosophy, and economics—books he had missed by going to Sandhurst rather than to Oxford or Cambridge.

A little more than a year after Churchill had arrived in India, a small border war broke out with Pathan Afghan tribesmen on the North-West Frontier. Churchill's regiment was not involved, but he requested permission to join the expedition into the Swat

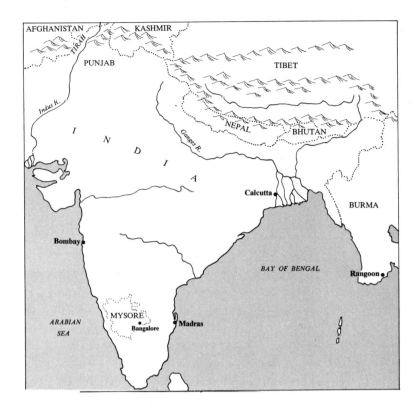

Winston Churchill's tour of duty in India.

Valley, where Alexander the Great had fought more than 2,200 years earlier. Before he left for the front Churchill again arranged to send periodic dispatches to a London newspaper.

After Churchill returned to his home station at Bangalore, he began his second career: He became a historian. His first published book was entitled *The Malakand Field Force*, about the campaign in which he had recently taken part. Since he felt that a historian should express opinions as well as record events, some of his military superiors called this book, when it was published in 1898, "A Subaltern's Hints to Generals."

Soon after the publication of his book, Churchill learned that a major British expedition was about to advance up the Nile into the Sudan, where the dervishes had a few years earlier captured Khartoum and killed its valiant garrison, including famous General Charles George "Chinese" Gordon. Since this was by far the most active British military operation then under way, Churchill felt that he must take part. With some difficulty, he obtained the approval of military superiors, who were beginning to have grave suspicions that this young writing soldier was too clever for his own good. He arrived in Cairo and joined the 21st Lancers. Again he was commissioned to act as a war correspondent for a London paper.

On September 1, 1898, Churchill led a troop of cavalry in the final charge which broke the resistance of the dervish army and won the Battle of Omdurman. This was one of the last cavalry charges of history.

Soon after the Omdurman campaign, Churchill decided that he could not afford to live on the pay of an army officer. His father, Lord Randolph, who had died three years earlier, had left barely enough money to support his widow. In those days, British army officers were usually members of the aristocracy, and were expected to have private incomes to maintain themselves in a way which would have been impossible on their meager pay. Since his writing had been so successful, Churchill decided that he would devote himself thenceforward to being an author.

Hardly had he returned to England when Churchill found himself drawn into the activity which was to become his princi-

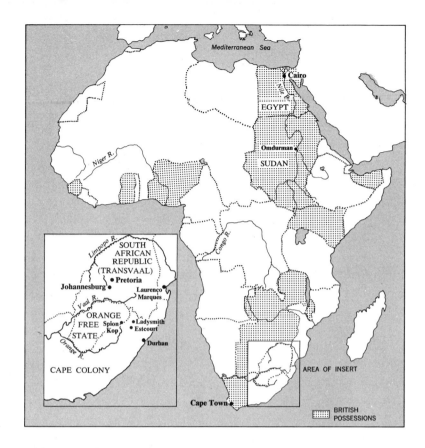

Africa, showing the areas of Winston Churchill's military experiences.

pal profession for the remainder of his days—politics. His first political campaign took place in late June and early July of 1899. He ran for Parliament in the borough of Oldham, near Manchester in central England, as a member of the Conservative party. He lost.

The sting of political defeat was eased by the publication shortly thereafter of his book, *The River War*, on the Nile campaign. This received very favorable reviews and became a best seller. Churchill could take solace from the fact that although he could not afford to be a soldier, and apparently did not yet have the capability to be a politician, at least he could support himself and, by writing, gain the fame that he craved.

The Boer War

In October of 1899, war broke out in South Africa. Two small Boer (or Dutch) nations, the Transvaal Republic and the Orange Free State, declared war against Great Britain, following long and inconclusive disputes. Churchill, as a civilian war correspondent, accompanied the first expeditionary force that sailed from Britain a few weeks later.

In November, soon after arriving in South Africa, Churchill accompanied a force attempting to relieve the besieged city of Ladysmith, in British Natal. He was captured in a Boer ambush, and sent to a prison camp in Pretoria, capital of the Transvaal Republic. The Boers paid no attention to his claim that, as a civilian war correspondent, he should not be treated as a prisoner of war. On December 12 he escaped, and after a series of dramatic and thrilling adventures, reached the seaport of Lourenço Marques in Portuguese East Africa. From there, he took a ship to Durban, capital of Natal, where he was hailed as a hero. As he wrote later: "The Admiral, the General, the Mayor pressed on board to grasp my hand. Borne along on the shoulders of the crowd, I was carried to the steps of the town hall, where nothing would content them but a speech, which after a becoming reluctance I was induced to deliver."

This historic photo shows Churchill among a group of British prisoners during the Boer War at a camp in South Africa in 1899. Less than a month after his capture, Churchill made headlines with his daring escape. (UPI)

Peace and Politics

By the fall of 1900, after most of the regular fighting in South Africa was ended, Churchill returned to England to find himself a national hero. Having acquired fame, the dashing young man with red-golden hair was easily elected to Parliament early in 1901. Always a man of decided opinions, and never reluctant to express them, he began to disagree with many of the

Churchill is shown here in British Army uniform in 1900. (UPI)

Conservative party's policies. In 1904 in a speech in the House of Commons, he dramatically withdrew from the Conservative party, and joined the opposition Liberals. The aristocratic Conservatives were shocked. It was incredible to them that a member of one of the best families of Britain could become, as they believed, a traitor to his class; he found himself a social outcast in the eyes of many of his former friends.

Churchill's new political career did not stop him from writing. In 1906 he published a biography of his father, *Life of Lord Randolph Churchill.* Scholars and popular critics alike hailed it; Winston Churchill was clearly a serious writer and an accepted historian, not merely a journalist and writer of adventures. The pattern that was to mold his future life was com-

10

pleted two years later when he married Miss Clementine Hozier; as he later wrote in one of his books, "I married and lived happily ever afterwards."

In 1906 Churchill had been appointed to his first government position as Undersecretary of State for the Colonies. He entered the Cabinet in 1908 as President of the Board of Trade. In those days this position had responsibilities similar to those which are today shared in the United States by the Secretaries of Labor, Commerce, and Transportation. His brilliant performance led to his appointment in 1910 as Home Secretary, responsible for the internal administration of the United Kingdom.

Churchill with his bride, a week before their marriage in 1908. (UPI)

As a member of the Cabinet, Churchill became concerned with British foreign policy, which was then focused on relations with Germany. In 1904, the growing naval power of Germany, combined with an increasingly aggressive German foreign policy, had caused Britain to enter into an alliance with France. This had been expanded in 1907 into the Triple Entente, an alliance among three ancient enemies—Britain, France, and Russia—to offset the powerful Triple Alliance of Germany, Austria-Hungary, and Italy.

At first, Churchill did not believe that German ambitions endangered the peace of Europe. In general, as a member of Parliament and as a Cabinet officer, he opposed measures to increase the strength or financing of the army and the navy. But in the summer of 1911, German threats against France, and particularly the Agadir Incident in which Germany tried to end French colonial influence in Morocco, caused Churchill to change his mind. Realizing that the powerful nations of Europe had been on the verge of mobilization, he became convinced that Britain should increase her military strength in order to deter Germany from any further expansionist adventures. If deterrence failed, then Britain would be better prepared to wage war. He began an intensive study of the existing military situation in Europe, and spent all his spare time in reading about current and historical military affairs.

During the final weeks of the Agadir crisis, Churchill, the Home Secretary, suddenly and unexpectedly produced for the

Prime Minister and the Committee of Imperial Defence an amazing memorandum entitled "Military Aspects of the Continental Problem." Dated August 13, 1911, this document was a dispassionate, precise paper of the sort which a General Staff would call either an "estimate of the situation" or a "staff appreciation." Churchill's purpose in writing the paper was to estimate the manner in which Britain's relatively small forces could influence major operations on the Continent if war were to break out.

Although Churchill was completely ignorant of the German Schlieffen Plan, his own shrewd estimates of the German strategic problem, and the manner in which the Germans would respond to it, were amazingly precise. He demonstrated that current French plans for an offensive against Germany in the first weeks of the war were totally unrealistic. As he wrote, "The balance of probability is that by the twentieth day [after the beginning of mobilization] the French armies will have been driven back from the Line of the Meuse and will be falling back on Paris and the South. All plans based upon the opposite assumption ask too much of fortune. . . . [A force of] four or six British divisions in these great initial operations . . . [would be of] value to the French . . . out of all proportion to its numerical strength. It would encourage every French soldier and make the task of the Germans in forcing the frontier much more costly. But . . . France will not be able to end the war successfully by any action on the frontiers. She will not be strong enough to invade Germany. Her only chance is to conquer Germany in France. . . .

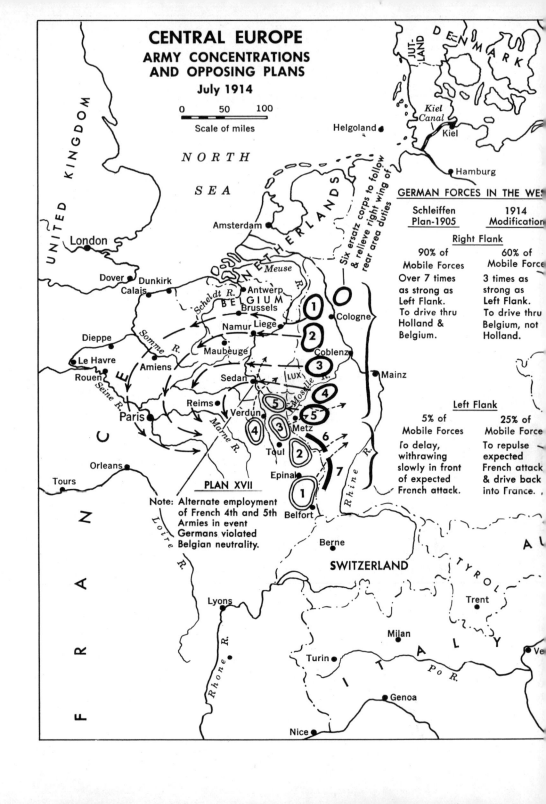

CENTRAL EUROPE
ARMY CONCENTRATIONS AND OPPOSING PLANS
July 1914

0   50   100
Scale of miles

JUT-LAND
DENMARK

Kiel Canal
Kiel

Helgoland

Hamburg

NORTH SEA

NETHERLANDS

Amsterdam

Meuse R.

Six ersatz corps to follow & relieve right wing of rear area duties

GERMAN FORCES IN THE WES

Schleiffen Plan-1905	1914 Modification
Right Flank	
90% of Mobile Forces Over 7 times as strong as Left Flank. To drive thru Holland & Belgium.	60% of Mobile Force 3 times as strong as Left Flank. To drive thru Belgium, not Holland.
Left Flank	
5% of Mobile Forces To delay, withrawing slowly in front of expected French attack.	25% of Mobile Force To repulse expected French attack & drive back into France.

UNITED KINGDOM

London

Dover
Calais
Dunkirk

Scheldt R.
BELGIUM
Antwerp
Brussels
Namur   Liege

Cologne

①
② Coblenz
③
Mainz

Dieppe

Somme R.
Maubeuge

Le Havre
Amiens
Rouen

Seine R.

Sedan   LUX

Moselle R.

④
⑤
⑤

Reims
Verdun
Marne R.

Metz

④ ③

Paris

Toul
②

6

Orleans

Epinal

Rhine R.

7

Tours

PLAN XVII

Note: Alternate employment of French 4th and 5th Armies in event Germans violated Belgian neutrality.

①
Belfort

Loire R.

Berne

SWITZERLAND

AU

TYROL

Trent

FRANCE

Rhone R.

Lyons

Milan

Turin

ITALY

Po R.

Ve

Genoa

Nice

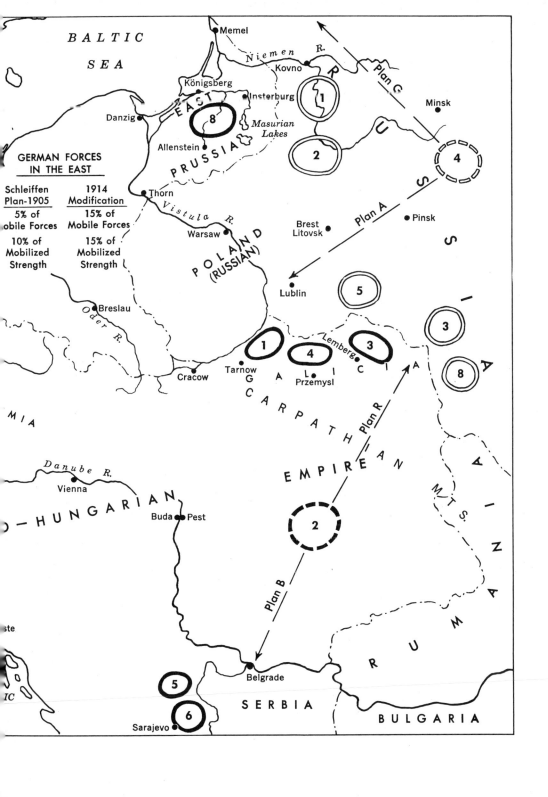

BALTIC

SEA

Memel

Niemen R.

Kovno

Königsberg

Insterburg

Danzig

EAST

PRUSSIA

Allenstein

Masurian Lakes

Minsk

Plan G

R

U

S

Plan A

Pinsk

4

1

8

2

GERMAN FORCES
IN THE EAST

Schleiffen Plan-1905	1914 Modification
5% of obile Forces	15% of Mobile Forces
10% of Mobilized Strength	15% of Mobilized Strength

Thorn

Vistula R.

Warsaw

POLAND
(RUSSIAN)

Brest Litovsk

Lublin

5

Breslau

Oder R.

Cracow

Tarnow

G A L I C I A

Lemberg

Przemysl

1

4

3

3

8

CARPATHIAN

MIA

Danube R.

Vienna

O-HUNGARIAN

Buda Pest

EMPIRE

Plan R

MTS.

ste

IC

5

Belgrade

Plan B

2

RUMANIA

6

Sarajevo

SERBIA

BULGARIA

"By the fortieth day Germany should be extended at full strain both internally and on her war fronts, and this strain will become daily more severe and ultimately overwhelming, unless it is relieved by decisive victories in France. If the French Army has not been squandered by precipitate or desperate action, the balance of forces should be favourable after the fortieth day, and will improve steadily as the time passes."

These views were completely contrary to the estimates and war plans of the French General Staff and to similar estimates prepared by the British General Staff. In fact, General Henry Wilson, the Director of Military Operations in the British War Office, called Churchill's memorandum "silly." Nevertheless, three years later these assertions were proven completely correct. Through logic, through thorough study of the military situation in Europe and in Great Britain, and through a process of analysis which was probably the genesis of the modern "operations research"—and aided by a flair for strategic genius—Churchill had produced one of the most accurate and most profound strategic analyses to be found in the records of history.

CHAPTER 2

First Lord of the Admiralty

Greatly impressed by Churchill's understanding of the military situation in Europe and of Britain's military posture, in August, 1911, the Prime Minister, Sir Herbert Asquith, appointed him a member of the Committee of Imperial Defence. On October 25, 1911, Asquith made him First Lord of the Admiralty (comparable to the American Secretary of the Navy). The new First Lord applied to his naval responsibilities the same kind of penetrating analysis he had recently given to the subject of mobilization of land armies in Europe.

Churchill was no stranger to naval affairs. In 1907 he had formed a close friendship with the man who had completely revolutionized the British navy, and with it naval warfare. This was Admiral of the Fleet Sir John Fisher, who was then First Sea Lord (the equivalent of the American Chief of Naval Operations), who had designed the dreadnought, the all big-gun battleship. In addition to intensive reading on naval affairs and naval history, Churchill kept himself abreast of all that was going on in naval warfare by frequent long talks with Lord Fisher—the title awarded him after he retired as First Sea Lord in 1910. And so, when Churchill came to the Admiralty, he had in mind the need for many reforms.

First and most important was the new First Lord's belief that the basic war plans of the Royal Navy were antiquated, with no appreciation of the impact of new weapons on naval warfare.

The principal reason for Napoleon's downfall a century earlier had been the Royal Navy's tenacious and close blockade of the ports of Europe from 1803 to 1814. The importance of naval blockade had been reinforced in the minds of British naval leaders by the Union Navy's successful close blockade of Southern ports in the American Civil War. A close blockade of German ports was the principal element of the British war plan in 1911.

Churchill was a firm believer in the importance of blockade, but he was convinced that the torpedo, the submarine, and possibly aircraft would make it impossible to carry out a close blockade of continental ports. He felt that any effort to do so would result in such heavy losses that either the blockade would have to be abandoned, or the weakened navy would be overwhelmed in battle by the German fleet. It seemed to him, looking at a map of Northwestern Europe, that Germany could best be blockaded from a distance, by closing off the entrances to the North Sea at the Straits of Dover and in the narrow seas between northern Scotland and Norway. He was completely unconcerned when international lawyers told him there was no precedent for a distant blockade, and that efforts to enforce it would violate the international rights of freedom of the seas.

This question of naval strategy was only one of several

The Right Honorable Winston Spencer Churchill, First Lord of the Admiralty. (National Archives)

problems with which Churchill was concerned. He realized that it could not be settled without attacking some of the others first. These were, as he was to write later, as follows:

Second, the organisation of the fleets with a view to increasing their instantly ready strength. Third, measures to guard against all aspects of surprise in the event of a sudden attack. Fourth, the formation of a Naval War Staff. Fifth, the concerting of the War Plans of the Navy and the Army by close co-operation of the two departments. Sixth, further developments in design to increase the gun power of our new ships in all classes. Seventh, changes in the high commands of the Fleet and in the composition of the Board of the Admiralty.

19

Reorganizing the Admiralty

Shortly after Churchill became First Lord, he completely reorganized the Admiralty and its procedures, carefully watching all of his naval assistants to see how they reacted to his new .measures. Although the threat of war as a result of the Agadir Incident seemed to be receding, he put the Admiralty on a twenty-four-hour operational basis, with clerks and duty officers available to take instant action in the event of an emergency after duty hours. He installed a war chart on the wall behind his desk, on which the location of all German warships was to be marked every day. At every opportunity—traveling by the Admiralty yacht, by railroad, or by automobile—he visited every important naval installation in Great Britain. Not only did he wish to make himself aware of the state of readiness of the fleet and to meet and to evaluate all of the senior officers of the navy, he also was determined to impress upon the entire navy his own concern about the ever-present threat posed to Britain by steadily increasing German naval power.

In these intensive and revitalizing efforts Churchill called for assistance from his old friend Lord John Fisher. Although some of the things that Churchill was changing were policies and practices that Fisher himself had initiated, the old admiral agreed with almost everything that Churchill was doing. Fisher gave wise and sound advice on actions to be taken, policies to be adopted, and officers to be selected for important commands.

The relationship between these two close friends, the retired old sea dog and the young political administrator, was not always smooth. Nevertheless, when Churchill felt that he needed advice or comment on matters of strategy or organization, and above all on the design, protection, and armament of warships, he would turn to Fisher. One typical letter from Fisher to Churchill contained the following passages:

> *Don't make any mistake about big submarines being obligatory*! Big risks bring big success! . . . Increased surface speed is *above all* a necessity. . . . Battle tactics will be revolutionised. . . . For God's sake trample on and stamp out protected Cruisers and hurry up Aviation. . . .

Churchill did not need any suggestions from Fisher to realize the potential importance of aircraft to warfare. In the early months of 1914 he himself learned how to fly.

Churchill was particularly concerned about the need for something like a General Staff for the navy. He found most senior naval officers unalterably opposed to any such scheme. As he wrote:

> It takes a generation to form a General Staff. . . . The dead weight of professional opinion was adverse. They had got on well enough without it before. They did not want a special class of officer professing to be more brainy than the rest. . . . We had competent administrators, brilliant experts of every description, unequalled navigators, good disciplinarians, fine sea-officers, brave and devoted hearts: but at the outset of the conflict we had more captains of ships than captains of war. . . . At least fifteen

years of consistent policy were required to give the Royal Navy that widely extended outlook upon war problems and of war situations without which seamanship, gunnery, instrumentalisms of every kind, devotion of the highest order, could not achieve their due reward.

Fifteen years! And we were only to have thirty months!

Thirty Months of Accomplishment

It was a bare thirty-two months from the time that Churchill arrived at the Admiralty until Europe was shaken by the assassination of Archduke Franz Ferdinand of Austria at Sarajevo. As Europe teetered on the brink of war in July, 1914, Churchill could look back with considerable satisfaction on the progress that he had made.

By 1912, Churchill had instituted in the war plans the policy of distant blockade. The British Grand Fleet was to be based north of Scotland in the Orkney Islands at the protected anchorage of Scapa Flow. The southern exit from the North Sea was to be blocked at the Straits of Dover by minefields, as well as by destroyers and the heavy guns of older warships not fast enough to keep up with the Grand Fleet.

As to his second objective, Churchill and his new naval staff had substantially modified the organization of the fleet. He had also taken measures to improve the previously lax protection of British naval installations and supplies from possible sabotage on land.

The German Naval Challenge

During those thirty-two months, Churchill had perhaps devoted more time and effort to the sixth of his principal objectives than to any of the others. This was to improve the design of warships, and to increase the firepower of their weapons. The Germans had begun an intensive effort to build up their own fleet of dreadnoughts, with supporting cruisers and destroyers, to challenge British mastery of the seas. Through Britain's greater shipbuilding facilities, and by a grim national determination not to let Germany get ahead, the fighting strength of the Royal Navy was maintained at a strength at least half again as large as Germany's. But because of Britain's many overseas commitments around the world, Churchill did not think this margin was large enough. Furthermore he was concerned by the fact that German ships were being constantly improved in defensive strength, and their guns were being made more powerful. He had therefore thrown himself into an intensive effort to obtain the approval of Parliament for a shipbuilding program which would bring the number of British dreadnoughts to almost twice that which Germany could be expected to have. The program would improve the design of British ships and enable them to take more punishment from the heavy German weapons, and would in particular increase British naval firepower.

Turning frequently to Lord John Fisher for advice and support, Churchill had made great strides in these efforts. Particularly important were two strategic decisions. First, in order to get more speed ("Speed, speed, speed" was written time after time in Fisher's letters to Churchill) he had decided that future British warships should be fueled with oil rather than coal. Since Britain had no fuel-oil deposits, but was one of the world's largest producers of coal, this was a dangerous decision to make, politically and strategically. But Churchill felt that the advantage given to British warships by this additional speed warranted the risks. The other decision was to start building battleships carrying guns of 15-inch caliber, and firing projectiles weighing almost a ton, nearly twice as heavy as those that could be fired from the largest German gun. These were to be mounted in a new class of fast battleships, or superdreadnoughts, with a speed of 25 knots, which would enable them to keep up with battle cruisers.

The new organization and the new war plans were intensively tested in fleet maneuvers during the summers of 1912 and 1913. For the summer of 1914 Churchill, and his new First Sea Lord, Admiral Prince Louis of Battenberg, had planned a test mobilization to make certain that every possible man and ship would be ready to take a place in the war plan strategy within hours of a mobilization order.

War Clouds Over Europe

Although tensions between Austria and Serbia, and between the Triple Alliance and the Triple Entente, were growing in July, 1914, the test mobilization went according to plan. It be-

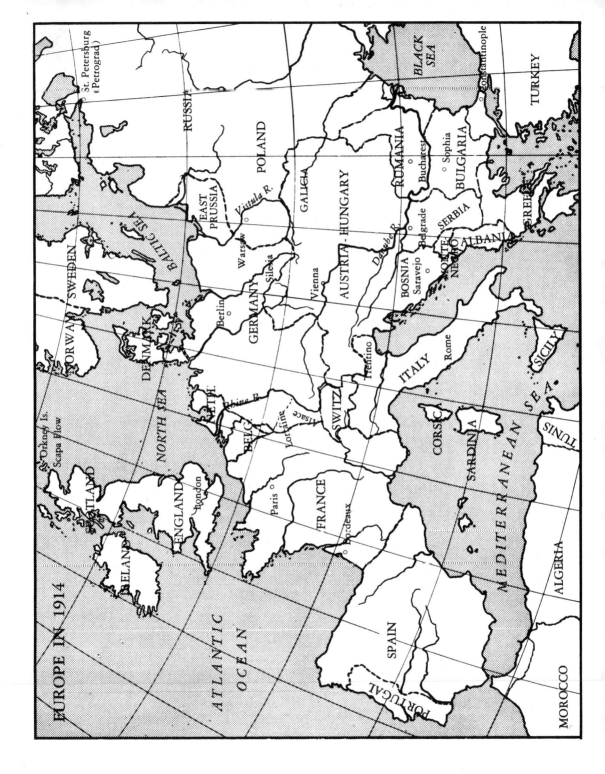

EUROPE IN 1914

MOROCCO

ATLANTIC OCEAN

IRELAND

SCOTLAND
Orkney Is.
Scapa Flow

ENGLAND
London

NORTH SEA

NORWAY

SWEDEN

BALTIC SEA

DENMARK

NETH.

BELG.

Rhine R.

Lorraine

Alsace

FRANCE
Paris
Bordeaux

SPAIN

PORTUGAL

SWITZ

GERMANY
Berlin

EAST PRUSSIA

Vistula R.

Warsaw

Silesia

POLAND

GALICIA

Vienna

AUSTRIA - HUNGARY

Danube R.

Trentino

ITALY
Rome

CORSICA

SARDINIA

MEDITERRANEAN SEA

ALGERIA

TUNIS

SICILY

RUSSIA

St. Petersburg (Petrograd)

RUMANIA
Bucharest

Sophia

BULGARIA

SERBIA
Belgrade

BOSNIA
Saravejo

MONTE NEGRO

ALBANIA

GREECE

BLACK SEA

Constantinople

TURKEY

gan on July 15, with the preparation and manning for combat of every ship of the Royal Navy, active and reserve. The test mobilization was completed with great success on July 23, and the ships began to go back to their normal peacetime status. By Friday, July 24, the reserve crews of the British Third Fleet (or reserve fleet) had gone home to their civilian pursuits. The more modern ships of the combined First and Second Fleets were scheduled to remain at Portland over the weekend. Then on Monday, the twenty-seventh, they would pay off the reserve members of their crews and go back to their scattered peacetime stations.

Churchill knew that the German High Seas Fleet was cruising off the coast of Norway, holding its usual summer maneuvers directly across the North Sea from Scotland. It seemed to him to present a direct menace to the security of Britain, while the world waited for Serbia's answer to the Austrian ultimatum.

The German fleet returned to its home bases before the weekend, but diplomatic tension increased in Central Europe. On July 26, with the approval of Churchill, who was at the seashore with his family, Prince Louis of Battenberg ordered the fleet not to disperse the following day. At the same time emergency measures for coastal defense were put into action. Churchill rushed back to London from his holiday, and on the twenty-seventh sent a message to British naval commanders around the world that war was "by no means impossible."

On July 28 came Austria's declaration of war on Serbia. That evening, on Churchill's orders and without consultation with the rest of the Cabinet, the Grand Fleet sailed from Portland, under the cover of darkness, and steamed through the Straits of Dover at high speed in a column 18 miles long. The fleet turned north, proceeding to Scapa Flow, where, if war came, it could control the approaches to Germany and protect the eastern and northern shores of Britain, while itself remaining secure from surprise attack. On July 29 Churchill received permission from the Cabinet to warn all British naval units, at home and scattered about the seven seas, to be alerted for war. That day he also ordered the seizure of all warships being built for foreign countries in British shipyards.

The Cabinet balked, however, on August 1 when Churchill requested permission to call up the reserves, to mobilize the Third Fleet and to bring the entire navy to a wartime footing. The majority of the British Cabinet still hoped that peace would be preserved, or that Britain could remain aloof from a continental struggle, despite her commitments to France and Russia.

Mobilizing the Navy

But that night, just before midnight, word was received in London that Germany had declared war on Russia. In a midnight meeting with the Prime Minister and a few other members of the Cabinet, Churchill announced that he would mobilize the reserve fleet; next day, Sunday, the assembled Cabinet approved.

On August 4, 1914, Britain delivered an ultimatum to Ger-

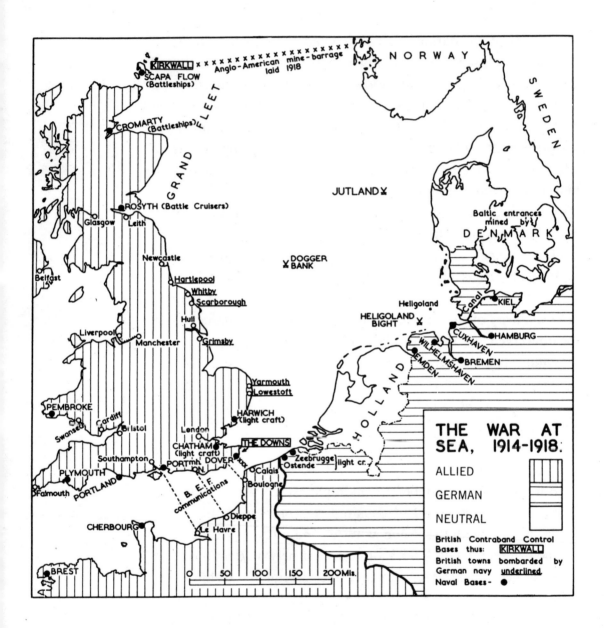

NORWAY

SWEDEN

× × × × × × × × × × × × × × × × × ×
Anglo-American mine-barrage
laid 1918

KIRKWALL ×
SCAPA FLOW
(Battleships)

GRAND FLEET

CROMARTY (Battleships)

JUTLAND ⚓

Baltic entrances
mined by

DENMARK

ROSYTH (Battle Cruisers)

Glasgow   Leith

Newcastle

Belfast

⚓ DOGGER
BANK

Canal   KIEL

Heligoland

HELIGOLAND
BIGHT ⚓

HAMBURG
CUXHAVEN
WILHELMSHAVEN
BREMEN
EMDEN

Hartlepool
Whitby
Scarborough

Hull

Liverpool
Manchester
Grimsby

HOLLAND

PEMBROKE
Swansea Cardiff Bristol

Yarmouth
Lowestoft

HARWICH
(light craft)

London

CHATHAM
(light craft)
DOVER
Calais
Boulogne

THE DOWNS

Zeebrugge
Ostende light cr.

Southampton
PORTMᵗʰ
PLYMOUTH
PORTLAND
Falmouth

B. E. F.
communications

Dieppe
Le Havre

CHERBOURG

BREST

0   50   100   150   200 Mls.

**THE WAR AT
SEA, 1914-1918.**

ALLIED

GERMAN

NEUTRAL

British Contraband Control
Bases thus: KIRKWALL
British towns bombarded by
German navy underlined.
Naval Bases ●

many: If the German invasion of Belgium were not halted by midnight, Britain would declare war upon Germany. At 11:00 P.M. that Tuesday, Churchill sat in the war room of the Admiralty listening to Big Ben, the clock in the tower of the houses of Parliament, strike the hour. It was midnight in Berlin. Churchill ordered the war message to be sent out to all British naval commanders throughout the world: "Commence hostilities against Germany." He then joined the Prime Minister and the remainder of the Cabinet at 10 Downing Street, to report that the message had been sent.

He could also report that the British fleet was fully deployed and mobilized for war, while the German fleet was still in port, only partly ready. It is clear from the record that Britain's complete readiness at sea, and a substantial measure of the naval superiority which the Royal Navy maintained over the German navy during the next four and one-half years, were due to the energy, the foresight, and the analytic brilliance of Winston Churchill.

CHAPTER 3

Winston at War

Moving the Army to France

In the following days and weeks Churchill took considerable satisfaction from the way in which the navy carried out its part in the joint war plans with the army. Between August 9 and 20, more than 100,000 British troops, four divisions, crossed the Channel to France. Every detail had been worked out so that train followed train to the Channel ports with the utmost precision, to be met by ships which then carried the troops and their equipment to France.

Not a single German destroyer or submarine sought to interfere, but if they had, they probably would not have succeeded. Cruisers patrolled north of the Straits of Dover, while masses of British submarines and destroyers stood guard just inside the straits. To the north and east squadrons of battleships, protected by their own cruisers and destroyers, steamed in readiness. And just in case the Germans tried to go around and approach from the west, more cruisers covered the western Channel approaches.

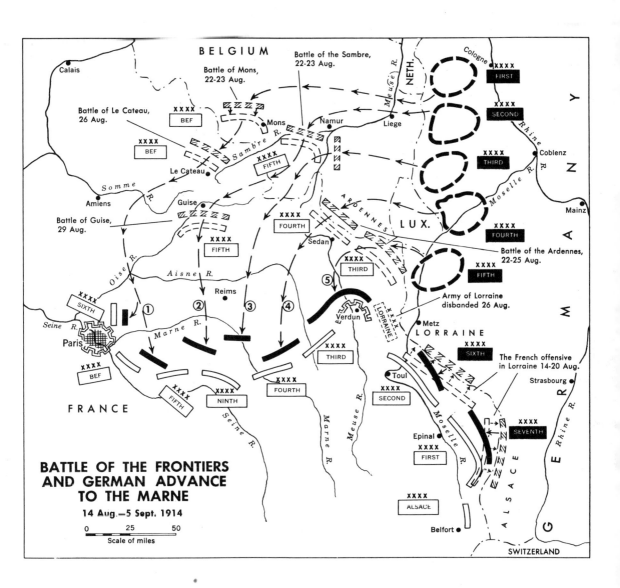

BELGIUM

Calais

Battle of Mons,
22-23 Aug.

Battle of the Sambre,
22-23 Aug.

NETH.

Cologne

XXXX
FIRST

Battle of Le Cateau,
26 Aug.

XXXX
BEF

Mons

Namur

Liege

XXXX
SECOND

Rhine R.

N

XXXX
BEF

Sambre R.

Le Cateau

XXXX
FIFTH

XXXX
THIRD

Coblenz

Moselle R.

Mainz

A

Somme R.

Amiens

Guise

XXXX
FOURTH

Sedan

ARDENNES

LUX.

XXXX
FOURTH

Battle of Guise,
29 Aug.

XXXX
FIFTH

Aisne R.

Reims

XXXX
THIRD

Battle of the Ardennes,
22-25 Aug.

XXXX
FIFTH

Oise R.

Seine R.

XXXX
SIXTH

①

②

③

④

⑤

Verdun

Army of Lorraine
disbanded 26 Aug.

Paris

Marne R.

**X X X
LORRAINE**

Metz

LORRAINE

XXXX
BEF

XXXX
THIRD

XXXX
SIXTH

The French offensive
in Lorraine 14-20 Aug.

XXXX
FIFTH

XXXX
NINTH

XXXX
FOURTH

Seine R.

Marne R.

Meuse R.

Toul

XXXX
SECOND

Strasbourg

FRANCE

Epinal

Moselle R.

XXXX
SEVENTH

XXXX
FIRST

Rhine R.

G

**BATTLE OF THE FRONTIERS
AND GERMAN ADVANCE
TO THE MARNE**

14 Aug.—5 Sept. 1914

0   25   50
Scale of miles

XXXX
ALSACE

Belfort

ALSACE

SWITZERLAND

31

The presence of the British Expeditionary Force (BEF) in France and Belgium so soon after the outbreak of war was a complete surprise to the German army commanders. The German plans for advancing into France were disrupted by the necessity of contending with this unexpected force of superb fighting men of the British Regular Army. There were many reasons for the German loss of the Battle of the Marne, but one of the most important was the presence of the BEF in the Battles of the Frontiers, and its movement into the gap between the German First and Second Armies on the critical day of the Battle of the Marne, September 9, 1914.

The next day Field Marshal Sir John French, Commander in Chief of the BEF, took time out to write a letter to Churchill as his army completed the crossing of the Marne River. He had just received from Churchill a copy of the Home Minister's memorandum of August 13, 1911. French wrote: "What a wonderful forecast you made in 1911. . . . I have shown it to a few of my staff. I was afraid of Joffre's strategy at first and thought he ought to have taken the offensive much sooner, but he was quite right."

Ground and Air Responsibilities

Late in August, Churchill had agreed with the new Secretary of State for War, Field Marshal Lord Horatio Kitchener, that the navy would create a diversion along the coasts of Belgium and northern France. They hoped that this would worry and divert the attention of the main German forces streaming through Belgium toward Paris. Another purpose of this effort was to give moral support, at the very least, to the Belgian army, which had withdrawn to a defensive position in northwest Belgium, near Antwerp. Churchill sent a brigade of Royal Marines, only 3,000 strong, who landed at Ostend during the last week in August. For the next two weeks these marines followed Churchill's orders to give signs of great activity, in order to make the Germans think that at least a division was threatening their line of communications. This diversion did have some effect upon the Germans, but it did not cause them to make any great increase in their forces observing the Belgian army.

On September 3, Lord Kitchener told Churchill that German zeppelins had been sighted cruising over Antwerp and that German air attacks against London were to be expected. All of the army's airplanes had gone to France to support the BEF. In the years before the war, Churchill had established an efficient naval air service, despite the War Office protests that the army should be responsible for aerial home defense of Great Britain. Now Kitchener admitted the wisdom of Churchill's preparations, and asked if he would take responsibility for Britain's air defense.

Churchill was never reluctant to accept responsibility. Since the airplanes of 1914 could not climb to the same altitude as the German zeppelins, he decided to try to stop the threat at the source. He issued orders for attacks on known zeppelin sheds. But since his planes did not have enough range to reach far into

Germany from Britain, Churchill established air bases at Dunkirk and Calais.

At that time the Battle of the Marne was just beginning and there were no troops available to defend the British naval air bases against German cavalry raiders who had appeared in western Belgium and northern France. Having no cavalry, Churchill and his sailors decided to use automobiles, on which armor plate and machine guns were hastily mounted. By the middle of September, a ragged form of guerrilla warfare was taking place between German cavalry and the Royal Navy's armored cars in northern France and western Belgium.

The frustrated sailors soon discovered that their armored cars, although more speedy than the German horsemen, had certain shortcomings. Not only were they limited to the roads, but the German cavalry soon learned that they could block the cars by digging trenches across the roads. On September 23, 1914, Churchill wrote the following order to the director of his Air Division: "It is important that the . . . armed motor cars should be provided . . . with . . . the means of bridging small cuts in the road, and an arrangement of planks capable of bridging a ten- or twelve-feet span quickly and easily should be carried with every ten or twelve machines."

A few days later Churchill suggested the design of an armored vehicle which would carry a bridge in front which it could drop over a trench to cross and then pick up again. He was beginning to think in terms that would soon result in the concept of the tank.

On September 16, General Joffre had asked the British if

some marines could be sent to Dunkirk to reinforce the local garrison and make the Germans think that larger Allied forces were available in the north of France than actually were there. Churchill sent his brigade of Royal Marines to Dunkirk, along with fifty London buses. Using the buses, the marines traveled around through the northern tip of France and the western tip of Belgium, attracting as much attention as they could from German spies and from German cavalry raiders.

Antwerp

Following their defeat at the Marne, the main German armies retreated to the Aisne River, closely followed by the Allies. After inconclusive engagements along the Aisne, both the Allied and the German armies attempted to move around each other's open, western flank. This resulted in the rapid extension of trench lines first to the west and then to the north, through France toward the Belgian frontier, as each side vainly attempted to outflank the other. It soon became evident that, unless the approaching German right flank could be driven back, the Belgian army in and around Antwerp would be completely cut off from the British and French. The threatened Belgians prepared to evacuate Antwerp and to move westward toward Ostend and the French Channel coast.

The British were alarmed by the prospect that the Germans might be able to seize the important seaport of Antwerp, and much of the Belgian coast. Kitchener decided to land his two

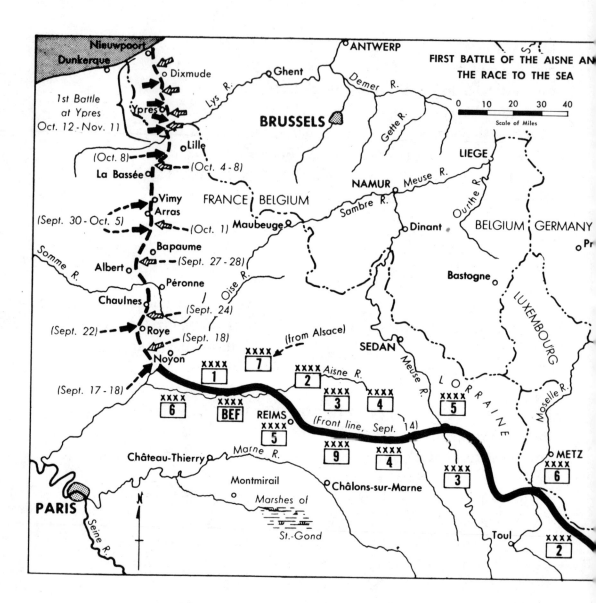

FIRST BATTLE OF THE AISNE AN
THE RACE TO THE SEA

Scale of Miles
0 10 20 30 40

1st Battle
at Ypres
Oct. 12 - Nov. 11

(Oct. 8)

(Oct. 4 - 8)

La Bassée

(Sept. 30 - Oct. 5)

Vimy
Arras

(Oct. 1)

Bapaume

(Sept. 27 - 28)

Albert

Péronne

Chaulnes

(Sept. 24)

(Sept. 22)

Roye

(Sept. 18)

Noyon

(from Alsace)

SEDAN

(Sept. 17 - 18)

XXXX
7

XXXX
1

XXXX
2

Aisne R.

XXXX
6

XXXX
BEF

REIMS

XXXX
3

XXXX
4

XXXX
5

(Front line, Sept. 14)

XXXX
5

Château-Thierry

XXXX
5

Marne R.

XXXX
9

XXXX
4

METZ

XXXX
6

PARIS

Montmirail

Marshes of
St.-Gond

Châlons-sur-Marne

XXXX
3

Toul

XXXX
2

Seine R.

Nieuwpoort
Dunkerque

Dixmude

Ghent

ANTWERP

Demer R.

Lys R.

BRUSSELS

Gette R.

LIEGE

Ypres

Lille

NAMUR

Meuse R.

FRANCE   BELGIUM

Sambre R.

Dinant

BELGIUM   GERMANY

Maubeuge

Pr

Bastogne

LUXEMBOURG

Somme R.

Oise R.

Ourthe R.

L O R R A I N E

Meuse R.

Moselle R.

36

remaining Regular Army divisions at Ostend, to link with the Belgians in Antwerp and the French troops moving north into Flanders in the "race to the sea." At the same time Sir John French's BEF was to be pulled out of the line on the Aisne River and sent northward by train to help in this desperate effort to hold all of Belgium west of the Scheldt River. To assist in this effort the British government believed that the Belgian government should be persuaded not to evacuate Antwerp.

Since Churchill had been particularly eloquent in Cabinet discussions about the importance of holding Antwerp, he was asked by his Cabinet colleagues to urge the Belgians not to withdraw. He was also authorized to take his marine brigade and some partly trained naval ground troops to Antwerp. It was hoped that this would convince the Belgians that the British were determined to support and reinforce them.

Churchill arrived in Antwerp on October 3, soon followed by his marines and two brigades of naval soldiers. The Belgians, who had intended to evacuate the city that day, were persuaded to stay. For five days the Belgian army, supported by Churchill's units, attempted to hold off the German forces slowly closing in around the city. By October 7, however, it was evident that the city could not be held much longer. As the Belgian army began to retreat to the west, Churchill also left the city and returned to London. The evacuation was completed on October 8.

Churchill has been much criticized for having left the Admiralty for nearly five days in order to command a not very effective division of marines and sailors in the unsuccessful defense of Antwerp. Unquestionably, he experienced an almost boyish enthusiasm in being under fire in the middle of a major battle, and at the same time carrying out an important personal role in persuading the Belgians to delay their withdrawal. But had Churchill not been there, the Belgians would have abandoned the city by October 4 or 5. As it was, when Sir John French's troops arrived at Ypres on October 12, they barely had time to get off their trains and deploy for battle against the Germans advancing from the east. In the bitter and momentous struggle of the following month, the German advance was halted by the desperate British defense of Ypres. Had Churchill not been at Antwerp, there would have been no Battle of Ypres, and German troops would have held the south shore of the Strait of Dover.

Continuing Naval Responsibilities

Despite his personal involvement at Antwerp, Churchill never forgot his larger responsibilities as First Lord of the Admiralty. Because of the efficient staff organization which he had created in the Admiralty, he was able to keep himself constantly informed on events around the world, and to take personal action to influence these events whenever he felt it necessary.

One of Churchill's principal worries in the early days of the war was the threat to the British sea-lanes posed by nine German cruisers scattered around the world. If they could simply be brought to battle, they would be overwhelmed. But until they were caught the German cruisers could threaten the flow of food and raw materials from overseas, which were necessary to feed the people of the United Kingdom and to provide British war industries with vital raw materials. Even more serious, these raiders could interfere with shipment of troops from British possessions and from the British dominions, so badly needed to replace the terrible casualties the British armies were suffering in Flanders.

For several months, this situation was alarming. German raiders terrorized the Indian Ocean, the South Atlantic, and much of the Pacific. When Japan entered the war and attacked the German colony at Tsingtao, Germany's China Squadron, under Admiral Maximilian von Spee, fled into the Central Pacific. Von Spee appeared unexpectedly off the west coast of South America, and on November 1 destroyed a small British squadron near Coronel, Chile.

Fisher Replaces Battenberg

There was another worry closer to home. Admiral Prince Louis of Battenberg, the First Sea Lord, had been under increasing—and very unfair—criticism because of his German birth. There was no more loyal British sailor in the Royal Navy than its senior admiral. But, on October 30, 1914, Prince Louis sadly told Churchill that he thought it would be in the best interest of Great Britain and of the Royal Navy if he resigned.

Churchill reluctantly accepted the resignation. He decided to call upon Lord Fisher to replace Lord Louis. Fisher was now seventy-three years old, but in excellent health, and with a mind as clear as it had been ten years before, when he had unveiled the dreadnought. At the same time, Churchill also called on another very distinguished retired admiral, Sir Arthur Wilson, to be a principal assistant to the First Sea Lord. Wilson had been First Sea Lord when Churchill came to the Admiralty in 1911. For the next six and one-half months, Fisher and Wilson provided the principal professional naval leadership in the Admiralty, complementing, and sometimes tempering, the less professional brilliance of their civilian superior.

The End of the German Raiders

When the news of the disaster of the Battle of Coronel reached London, on November 4, Churchill and his new First Sea Lord immediately surveyed the situation. The German cruisers had almost all the waters of the globe open to them, menacing trade routes and shipping everywhere. But after an analysis of the opportunities available to Admiral von Spee, Fisher told Churchill that he felt sure that the Germans would try to go eastward around Cape Horn. With Churchill's approval, he decided to strengthen the naval forces in the South Atlantic.

No one was more aware than Fisher of the need to maintain the strength of the Grand Fleet so that it would have a constant margin of superiority over the German High Seas Fleet, and he also realized that there had to be enough other ships to protect the British Isles and the main trade routes which fed the British people and British war industry. But Fisher decided that two battle cruisers could be spared; the *Invincible* and the *Inflexible* were ordered to the South Atlantic under Admiral Sir Doveton Sturdee.

On December 8, 1914, the day after Sturdee and his squadron arrived in the Falkland Islands, intending to take on coal and to search for the German ships, Admiral von Spee appeared with the intention of attacking the British naval base. The superior British naval squadron immediately steamed out, and in a six-hour battle sank four of the five German cruisers, and their two supply ships.

Meanwhile, all of the other German raiders had been sunk or blockaded. The one vessel that escaped from the Battle of the Falkland Islands was caught and destroyed by British ships on the west coast of South America early in 1915.

The Origins of the Tank

During the fall of 1914, Churchill spent twelve to eighteen hours in the Admiralty every day, save for his brief trips to Antwerp and northern France. He kept himself informed of every operation or activity going on at sea around the world, devoting particular attention to the North Sea. Yet he found time to maintain a steady correspondence with Sir John French, during the Battle of Ypres. He also kept himself as well informed as he could of operations taking place on the Eastern

An early British tank on exhibition in London. (National Archives)

Front, where the Russians were engaged in a series of mighty battles with the Germans and the Austro-Hungarians. But his active mind still had time to consider the new problems of land warfare, which had caused the stalemate on the Western Front—the unexpected deadliness of the firepower of artillery and machine guns, and the combination of these fearsome weapons with trenches and barbed wire.

Remembering the problems of his armored cars in Flanders, in October Churchill discussed the matter with the director of one of Britain's major ordnance factories. He asked if it would be possible to put armor plate on caterpillar tractors, which could carry guns and fighting men, and which could cross trenches by the endless belts of their tractor treads. The factory immediately began to develop a prototype vehicle which Churchill called a "land cruiser." While this work was going on, late in December Churchill learned that a British army officer, Colonel Ernest D. Swinton, had independently come up with a similar idea. Churchill at once endorsed Swinton's concept and wrote a memorandum to the Prime Minister about his own efforts to develop "land cruisers."

Lord Kitchener looked with favor upon Churchill's and Swinton's ideas, but the Ordance Department of the British War Ministry soon concluded that their proposals were impractical. Churchill, however, refused to let the matter drop. Since the army had turned the idea down, on February 20, 1915, Churchill established a "land ships committee" in the Admiralty. After receiving reports on two possible types of landships that would meet his requirements, he authorized development of prototypes, using Admiralty funds.

Churchill did not inform either the War Office or the Treasury of this action. As he later wrote: "It was a serious decision to spend [about £70,000] on a project so speculative, about the merits of which no high expert military or naval authority had been convinced. The matter, moreover, was entirely outside the scope of my own Department or of any normal powers which I possessed. Had the tanks proved wholly abortive or never been accepted or used in war by the military authorities, and had I been subsequently summoned before a Parliamentary Committee, I could have offered no effective defence to the charge that I had wasted public money on a matter which was not in any way my business and in regard to which I had not received expert advice from any responsible military quarter. The extremely grave situation of the war, and my conviction of the need of breaking down the deadlock which blocked the production of these engines, are my defence; but that defence is only valid in view of their enormous subsequent success."

In his memoirs on World War I, Churchill refused to claim credit for having invented the tank. "From very early times," he wrote, "the history of war is filled with devices of this character for use in the attack of fortresses and fortified positions." He does, however, assume the responsibility for initiating and sustaining the project, from which the first workable mechanized combat vehicles in history were to be produced, while giving full credit to the technicians and junior military officers who worked with him, and who developed the detailed designs. Beyond the shadow of a doubt, the man most responsible for the initiation of modern armored warfare was Winston Churchill.

CHAPTER 4

Strategic Problems
and the Dardanelles

Stalemate on the Western Front

By the beginning of December, 1914, two continuous, roughly parallel lines of fortification faced each other in Western Europe, zigzagging north from the Jura Mountains of northwestern Switzerland to the North Sea at Nieuport in Belgium. As time went on, during the next four deadly years, both lines of fortifications would be steadily improved and strengthened. But the basic pattern and nature of the defensive works were set before the end of 1914, as the front lines progressively stabilized from the southeast to the northwest.

The successful Battle of Ypres had come close to destroying Britain's splendidly trained but small Regular Army. At the beginning of the war there had been about 126,000 Regular troops in the British Isles, most of whom had gone to France. By the end of the year the BEF had suffered a total of 95,641 casualties. By 1915, territorial units (similar to the U.S. National Guard) and other reserve units were beginning to pour into France. Kitchener was raising and training a large volunteer army, but it would be at least six months before any of these would be ready for battle.

By the end of December, 1914, Churchill had come to the conclusion that the stalemate on the Western Front could not be broken without many more troops than Britain had available or without terrible casualties. It seemed to him that the logical thing for the Allies to do would be to go on the defensive in the West, at least until their supplies of ammunition and of trained manpower had been greatly built up, and to make use of Britain's command of the seas to strike at Turkey, Germany's weak, and relatively isolated, ally. He was strongly supported in this view by the dynamic Chancellor of the Exchequer, David Lloyd George.

It appeared to both Churchill and Lloyd George that if Turkey could be knocked out of the war, a sea-lane could be opened to Russia through the Turkish straits. This would also increase the economic pressure already being brought upon Germany through the blockade. Furthermore, once Turkey was eliminated, the Allies might then move to attack Austria-Hungary, which would be much easier to defeat than would Germany herself. Italy and the Balkan states had many grievances against the Austro-Hungarian Empire. Churchill and Lloyd George believed that when Turkey was eliminated from the war these nations of southern Europe would join the Allies in turning against the hated Austrians. Then, if Germany was not ready to make peace on terms that were favorable to the Allies, she would soon be overwhelmed by the combined strength of most of Europe.

"Westerners" vs. "Easterners"

Because they favored taking the offensive in the East against Turkey, Churchill, Lloyd George, and the others in the Cabinet who shared their views were called "Easterners." Their point of view was strongly opposed by most senior officers of the British army, as well as some of the Cabinet. These men, the "Westerners," felt that the Western Front, in France and Belgium, was the decisive theater of the war. They believed it would be a mistake to disperse any Allied troops elsewhere, in adventures that would have little direct effect upon Germany. Victory would come only when Germany, the principal enemy, was destroyed. The way to do this, the Westerners believed, was to build up overwhelming strength in France and to batter a gap in the German line of entrenchments, forcing the Germans either to retreat into their own country, or be destroyed by encirclement if they tried to stay in their positions in France and Belgium.

Lord Kitchener, the War Minister, had mixed feelings. He felt that it was absolutely essential that the British government give all possible support to the French government and to British troops in France. As an old soldier, he was well aware of the importance of psychological factors in war. Furthermore, he saw merit in the argument of the French government and of his own leading generals that the Western Front was the decisive front. But he also agreed with the logic of Churchill's arguments. If, as Churchill said, the navy had fighting forces that could not be used otherwise, Kitchener favored employing them against Turkey. He would be able to provide only a small land-force contingent, but this might be very useful in helping to knock Turkey out of the war. He gave cautious, although somewhat reluctant, approval of the Eastern strategy.

The feelings of brilliant, erratic Lord Fisher were even more mixed than those of Kitchener. Fisher was unalterably opposed to any effort anywhere that could possibly diminish the thin margin of dreadnought superiority which the Grand Fleet had over the German High Seas Fleet in the North Sea. Yet he agreed with Churchill that there were a number of old battleships that could not take their place in the battle line against the German navy, but that would be suitable for operations in the Eastern Mediterranean. He would have preferred an amphibious operation against the coast of Belgium, or possibly against the German naval base at Wilhelmshaven. But he was willing to agree to a joint operation against the Turkish Straits, provided that the army played a major role.

On December 29 in a memorandum for the Prime Minister, Churchill wrote:

> I think it quite possible that neither side will have the strength to penetrate the other's lines in the Western theatre. . . . The position of both armies is not likely to undergo any decisive change—although no doubt several hundred thousand men will be spent to satisfy the military mind on the point.
>
> For somewhat different reasons, a similar stalemate seems likely to be reached in the Eastern theatre. When the Russians come in contact with the German railway system, they are heavily thrown back. On the other hand,

withdrawn into their own country they can hold their own. . . .

How ought we to apply our growing military power? Are there not other alternatives than sending our armies to chew barbed wire in Flanders? Further, cannot the power of the Navy be brought more directly to bear upon the enemy? If it is impossible or unduly costly to pierce the German lines on existing fronts, ought we not, as new forces come to hand, to engage him on new frontiers, and enable the Russians to do so too? . . .

The action of the Allies proceeds almost independently. . . . We ought not to drift. . . . We ought to concert our action with our allies, and particularly with Russia. We ought to form a scheme for a continuous and progressive offensive, and be ready with this new alternative when and if the direct frontal attacks in France on the German lines and Belgium have failed, as fail I fear they will. Without your direct guidance and initiative, none of these things will be done; and a succession of bloody checks in the West and in the East will leave the Allies dashed in spirit and bankrupt in policy.

Churchill probably understood the nature of the Western Front stalemate better than did any other political or military leader on either side.

The Russian Plea for Help

The real debate between the Easterners and Westerners was precipitated in the first days of January, 1915. The Grand

Duke Nicholas, Commander in Chief of the Russian armies, sent an appeal to the British, to "arrange for a demonstration of some kind against [the] Turks." Russia, terribly hard pressed by the Germans and Austrians in Poland and Galicia, now found that her Caucasus frontier was threatened by a massive Turkish offensive. The situation was viewed with grave alarm by Lloyd George. He urged action to rally Greece and Bulgaria to the Allied cause in order to keep Turkey isolated from the other Central Powers and to relieve Serbia as well as Russia from the pressure of Germany and Austria-Hungary.

At about this same time, Kitchener asked Churchill what the navy could do to help him respond to the request of the Grand Duke Nicholas. Kitchener pointed out that he had no troops to spare for an attempt to force the Strait of the Dardanelles, but felt that it was essential that some sort of demonstration be carried out. He hoped that a naval bombardment of the Dardanelles forts would at least be part of this demonstration.

Fisher's Dardanelles Recommendation

The next day, January 3, 1915, Admiral Fisher strongly endorsed the idea of an operation against Turkey, with an army expedition of 75,000 troops, while the navy, using old battleships, would force its way through the Dardanelles. Fisher ended his memorandum to Churchill with these words: "But as the great Napoleon said, 'Celerity'—without it—'Failure'!"

In the light of subsequent events, it is indeed interesting that the first recommendation for a naval assault against the Dardanelles to be found in the records was written by Lord John Fisher. In the context, he was clearly suggesting an independent naval operation to be initiated as soon as possible, with the army troops committed as they became available.

On the basis of the general agreement now evident among Lloyd George, Sir Edward Grey (the Foreign Secretary), Kitchener, Fisher, and members of his naval staff, Churchill sent a radio message to Vice Admiral Sir Sackville Hamilton Carden, commanding British naval forces in the Eastern Mediterranean: "Do you consider the forcing of the Dardanelles by ships alone a practicable operation? . . . Importance of results would justify severe loss."

Two days later, on January 5, came Carden's reply: "I do not consider Dardanelles can be rushed. They might be forced by extended operations with large number of ships."

After a War Council meeting that afternoon, and following further discussions with members of his naval staff, Churchill sent an order to Admiral Carden to produce a detailed plan for "extended operations."

On January 11, Carden's plan arrived by radio in the Admiralty. He envisaged a deliberate step-by-step advance of the fleet through the Dardanelles. Carden felt that it might take a month for the fleet to blast its way through the strait, silencing the Turkish forts on either side; but he believed that with twelve old battleships and a number of lighter vessels, the task was feasible. He warned that the expenditure of ammunition would be large.

There are widely varying versions of how this plan was received in the Admiralty. Churchill was pleased, and he indicates that his reaction was shared by his senior staff advisers. But there is evidence that some of these, beginning with Lord Fisher himself, were now having second thoughts about the feasibility of a naval operation through the Strait of the Dardanelles, without any direct army assistance.

Since there were apparently no immediate or direct objections raised against the Carden plan, or against Churchill's endorsement of it, it is possible that the doubts which are mentioned in some memoirs really reflect reactions long after the event, and influenced by later developments. Admiral Sir Henry Jackson, Chief of the Admiralty War Staff, specifically approved the plan, and there was at first no indication of opposition from either Admiral Fisher or Admiral Wilson, the two senior officers in the Admiralty. The extent of the War Staff's support, in fact, is evidenced by its recommendation that the new superdreadnought HMS *Queen Elizabeth*, just commissioned, should test her unprecedentedly large 15-inch guns against the Dardanelles fortresses. This ship and her guns would be a tremendous addition to Admiral Carden's firepower.

At this time, Captain Herbert Richmond, a member of the War Staff, wrote: "With our modern, long heavy guns we can outrange the Turkish forts and a useful bombardment can be carried out. If we can force the passage, we have Constantinople open, and the results will, I hope, be a revolution in Turkey." Later Richmond was to be the greatest critic of the operation and of Churchill's role in it.

At a meeting of the War Council on January 13, the Carden Plan was presented by Churchill and was approved. Accompanying Churchill to the meeting, and supporting him in the presentation of the plan, were Admirals Fisher and Wilson. "The Admiralty," said the War Cabinet decision, "should . . . prepare for a naval expedition in February to bombard and take the Gallipoli Peninsula with Constantinople as its objective." The necessary orders were sent to Admiral Carden.

It was not until after this decision had been made, and preparations had been begun, that Admiral Fisher began to express doubts regarding the expedition. In a later War Council meeting he voiced reluctance to risk ships in an attack on land fortifications without land-force support. But, on January 28, after Churchill and the Prime Minister tried to pin him down to specific objections, Lord Fisher finally agreed to wholehearted participation.

The Assault on the Dardanelles

The Straits of the Dardanelles and of the Bosphorus, connected by the Sea of Marmara, separate the small portion of Turkey which lies in Europe from the larger part in Asia. The Mediterranean mouth of the Dardanelles, at Cape Helles, is 4,000 yards wide. The strait gradually widens to about 8,000 yards, then closes in again at the Narrows, 14 miles from the mouth, to a width of only 1,600 yards. Here Xerxes had crossed into Europe in the fifth century B.C. on a bridge of boats. Beyond the Narrows the strait slowly widens, and after the town of Gallipoli, some 40 miles from the mouth, opens into the Sea of Marmara.

The Turks had concentrated seventy-eight guns in eleven forts at the Narrows. Another twenty-four guns were in the forts that guarded the entrance. A few other forts were scattered along the remainder of the strait. After British ships shelled the outer forts in early November, 1914, the defenses were strengthened by a number of German howitzers, mobile guns that could be moved from one spot to another. A system of minefields was also set up in the main ship channel in the Narrows; these were protected by rapid-fire batteries and illuminated by powerful searchlights at night.

By mid-February Admiral Carden had assembled a force of sixteen old battleships (four of them French), one battle cruiser, and the superdreadnought *Queen Elizabeth* at Mudros, on the island of Lemnos. Two battalions of Royal Marines were stationed there to provide a landing party.

The desirability of sending a larger land force was meanwhile being discussed in London. Lord Fisher believed that land forces should seize the Gallipoli Peninsula after the fleet had battered its forts into submission. On February 16, the War Council decided that the 29th Division should be sent from England and that a force from Egypt should also be sent to Lemnos as soon as possible. General Sir Ian Hamilton was to command this land force. Three days later Lord Kitchener changed his mind and ordered the 29th Division to stay in England. Then, after the naval attack had started, Kitchener changed his mind again, and the 29th Division was sent to join the contingent from Egypt.

Bombardment of the Turkish forts at the entrance to the Dardanelles commenced at long range on the morning of February 19. The Turkish forts were not seriously damaged by this long-range bombardment, and Carden realized that the ships must move closer. But five stormy days of rough seas, bitter sleet, and snow prevented further attack until February 25. Meanwhile, in Constantinople, confusion reigned. Many people, including German advisers, thought that the British fleet would break through.

When the naval bombardment was resumed on February 25, the outer defense guns were quickly silenced. Parties of marines were landed on opposite sides of the entrance to the strait, and destroyed twenty of the Turkish guns without any interference. In the following days, the landing parties took care of thirty more Turkish guns. Long-range bombardment beyond the entrance continued sporadically and with some effect, while the British naval commander wrestled with the problem of how to get through the minefields at the Narrows.

Carden believed that the mines should be swept first so that the battleships could move in close to silence the heavy Turkish batteries. The minesweepers that accompanied the fleet were actually fishing trawlers from the north of England, with their own civilian crews. Inexperienced and poorly equipped for the task, these crews were most reluctant to enter the mined area, where the hazards of accidental explosion were multiplied by the menace of shore-based guns. When the civilian crews balked, and an attempt to sweep the fields with volunteer navy crews failed, Admiral Carden reversed his plans. He decided to make a concerted attack on the shore defenses first. But on March 17, the day before the attack was to take place, Carden collapsed from the strain. He was replaced by his second-in-command, Rear Admiral J.M. de Robeck.

Repulse at the Narrows

In accordance with plans, the next morning the fleet steamed up the Dardanelles about halfway to the Narrows. As the battleships advanced they kept up a heavy fire on the Narrows forts. The counterfire from the shore batteries was not very effective, although one French ship was badly damaged. As the Allied vessels approached the area of known minefields, the bombardment from the naval guns began to have its desired effect; fire from the forts slackened. De Robeck ordered the battleships to withdraw slightly, and the minesweepers advanced under the cover of their fire.

At this point the French battleship *Bouvet* suddenly hit a mine, or was hit by a shell—no one knows for sure—and sank within one minute with most of her crew. Soon after this, two old British battleships, *Ocean* and *Irresistible*, also went down.

The minesweepers meanwhile proceeded up the strait, but a few of the Turkish field guns opened fire again. The mine-

56

NAVAL ATTACK ON THE DARDANELLES
MARCH 18th., 1915

■ Hamidieh II   Principal Turkish Batteries
□   Turkish Minefield Batteries
●   Turkish Mobile Howitzer Batteries
◖   Allied Warships of line A
◗   Supporting Warships
◻   Allied Warships of line B
..50..   Turkish Minefields, giving number of mines
○   Searchlights

Nagara
Anadolu
Derma
Namazieh
Chemenlik
Chanak
Kilid Bahr
Hamidieh II →
Medjidieh →
Yildiz
Hamidieh I

GALLIPOLI

PENINSULA

Messudieh

Sari Sighlar
Bay

Kephez
Bay

Dardanos

Prince
George
Queen Elizabeth
Agamemnon
Lord Nelson
Helles
Majestic
Gaulois
Charlemagne
Inflexible
Sedd-el-Bahr
Vengeance
Bouvet
Irresistible
Triumph
Albion
Ocean
Suffren
Swiftsure
Kum Kale
Eren Keui Bay

N

0   4000
Yards

57

sweeper crews panicked and withdrew. De Robeck was now convinced that the fleet could not hope to run through the minefields without further losses. In the late afternoon he ordered a withdrawal.

The Allies had lost three battleships, three more were crippled, and almost seven hundred sailors had perished. Although the Turkish guns had been silenced by the hail of naval shells, it was later learned that only forty Turks had been killed and seventy wounded, and four guns destroyed. However, the Turks' supply of ammunition for their long-range guns had been almost entirely expended, although the British did not know this at the time.

Neither Churchill nor Fisher considered that the loss of three battleships was excessive or unexpected. Other ships were sent to join the fleet, and de Robeck was ordered to push ahead. But on March 22, General Hamilton and Admiral de Robeck met on the *Queen Elizabeth* and agreed that the Straits could not be forced without support from the army. They so reported in a radio message to London.

Churchill was disappointed by this report, and was prepared to order de Robeck to continue with his attacks. However, his top naval advisers, Lord Fisher and Admirals Wilson and Jackson, refused to agree. Fisher pointed out to Churchill that they must accept the considered views of the commander on the spot.

Delay and Inaction

The Prime Minister was as disappointed as Churchill with this state of affairs, and the two political leaders were appalled as day followed day with de Robeck doing nothing to maintain pressure on the Turks or to resume the bombardment. But Asquith refused to issue orders overriding the advice of the military professionals. For more than a month there was no activity at the Dardanelles, while the army prepared its expedition in Alexandria, Egypt.

When on March 23 Churchill had announced to the War Council that de Robeck had called off his attacks and that the Admiralty staff supported him in this decision, Lord Kitchener said that he would continue the operation with land forces. But in the following weeks both Kitchener and Hamilton seemed to feel that the navy had completely abandoned the operation, and had transferred all responsibility to the army. Although Churchill was pleased that the army was now involved, as he and Fisher had desired from the outset, he was frustrated both by the long delays of army preparation and by the inactivity of his own naval forces.

Had the Allies been ready to land on Gallipoli immediately, the outcome would probably have been a quick occupation of the peninsula and the opening of the Narrows to the fleet. The marine landing parties had met no opposition. But the delay of more than a month between the naval attacks and the army landings was sufficient to permit the Turks to strengthen their defenses greatly. The British fleet made no attempt to interfere.

The Allied landings on the tip of the Gallipoli Peninsula on April 25 encountered fierce Turkish opposition. Despite fearful casualties, the British were able to get ashore but they made little headway. There was no naval action in the strait to support the landings, although there was some naval gunfire support against Turkish positions in front of the landing troops. Finally, on May 9, de Robeck agreed to another operation in the strait. But Fisher was by now absolutely opposed to any naval action in the strait area until the army had occupied the heights overlooking the Narrows. Over the objections of both Kitchener and Churchill, Fisher persuaded Prime Minister Asquith to approve the withdrawal of the *Queen Elizabeth*.

Kitchener was furious. At a meeting of the War Council two days later, on May 14, he complained that he had been let down by the navy. At this point Fisher spoke up to assert that he had been against the Dardanelles operation from the beginning. No one reminded him that he had been the first one to suggest it. The meeting was, as Churchill later wrote, "sulphurous." Not only had the operations in Gallipoli been most unsuccessful, and at heavy cost, but at the same time a major British offensive on the Western Front in France, at Souchez and Festubert, had been repulsed by the Germans with exceptionally severe losses.

Since Churchill had been the principal supporter of the Dardanelles operation, many of those present at the meeting considered him responsible for all the failures which had occurred. Churchill responded eloquently, and said he never

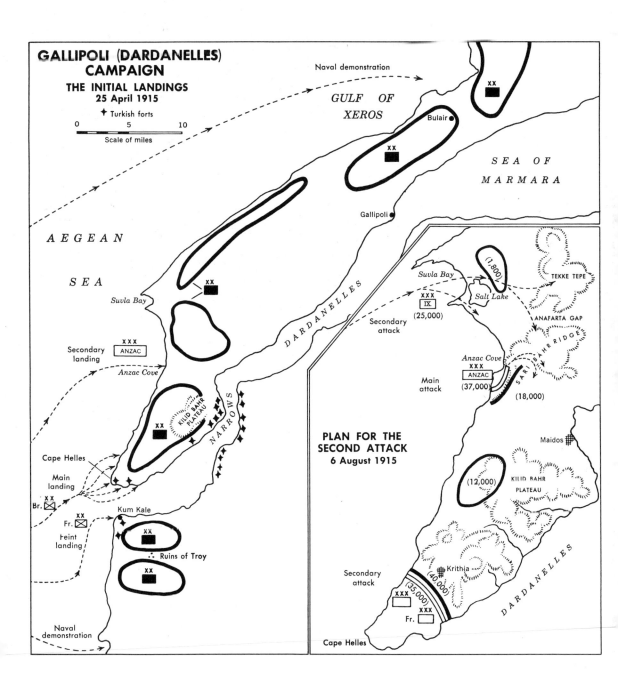

GALLIPOLI (DARDANELLES) CAMPAIGN

THE INITIAL LANDINGS
25 April 1915

✝ Turkish forts

0   5   10

Scale of miles

Naval demonstration

GULF OF XEROS

Bulair ●

SEA OF MARMARA

Gallipoli ●

A E G E A N

S E A

Suvla Bay

Secondary landing

XXX
ANZAC

Anzac Cove

DARDANELLES

N A R R O W S

KILID BAHR PLATEAU

Cape Helles

Main landing

XX
Br.

XX
Fr.

Kum Kale

Feint landing

∴ Ruins of Troy

Naval demonstration

Suvla Bay

(1,800)

TEKKE TEPE

XXX
IX
(25,000)

Salt Lake

ANAFARTA GAP

Secondary attack

SARI BAHR RIDGE

Anzac Cove

XXX
ANZAC
(37,000)

Main attack

(18,000)

Maidos

PLAN FOR THE SECOND ATTACK
6 August 1915

(12,000)

KILID BAHR PLATEAU

Secondary attack

(40,000)

● Krithia

XXX
(35,000)

XXX
Fr.

DARDANELLES

Cape Helles

Landing heavy guns on the Gallipoli Peninsula. Note the difficult terrain posed by the heights above. Turks could fire directly down on British troops. (National Archives)

would have endorsed an unsupported naval attack in March if he had known that two months later 80,000 troops would be available for fighting on the peninsula. But, he pointed out, it was too late to try to undo what had been done, and they must deal with the situation as it existed. He urged halting the offensive in France and concentrating all available reinforcement and ammunition to reach a decision at Gallipoli.

Fisher Resigns; Churchill Dismissed

That evening, after the War Council meeting, Churchill and Fisher had a friendly conversation. Next morning, however, the old First Sea Lord resigned. Then, in an amazing display of vindictiveness Fisher began direct personal attacks against Churchill. Not only did he denounce Churchill to the Prime Minister, but he also stimulated the opposition Conservative party in Parliament to insist on Churchill's dismissal from the Admiralty.

The Prime Minister gave way in the face of this pressure; he decided to form a coalition Cabinet and remove Churchill. Mr. Arthur James Balfour, a strong man and a loyal supporter of Churchill's, even though a member of the Conservative party, was appointed First Lord of the Admiralty, at Churchill's recommendation.

Before he had realized that he would be dismissed, Churchill had asked Admiral Sir Arthur Wilson if he would become First Sea Lord in Fisher's place. On May 19, however, when he had heard that Churchill was to be out, Wilson refused to accept the appointment. Balfour, and Asquith, tried to get him to change his mind. But Wilson wrote to the Prime Minister that "although I agreed to undertake the office of First Sea Lord under Mr. Churchill because it appeared to me to be the best means of maintaining continuity of policy under the unfortunate circumstances that have arisen, I am not prepared to undertake the duties under any new First Lord."

Churchill, who had never had the same close relationship with Wilson that he had had with Fisher, was both astonished and touched by this. He, too, tried to get Sir Arthur to reconsider, but the old admiral refused. He told Churchill, "You know all the moves on the board. I should only have to put the brake on from time to time. I could not possibly manage with anyone else."

Sir Arthur Wilson's attitude and actions show that he believed at that time what later study of the facts has revealed: Although Churchill was the chief supporter of the Dardanelles operation, he did not originate the idea of the naval assault, and was not responsible either for its failure or that of the subsequent land attack. These efforts were doomed by poor planning, poor support, and poor coordination. While no single man can be held responsible for the failures, if either of the operations had been conducted as Churchill recommended, it would probably have succeeded.

CHAPTER 5

Disgrace and Recovery

Inactivity in London

Churchill had not been fully aware of the strength of the opposition to him, and Asquith's announcement that he was to leave the Admiralty was a hard blow. He was touched, however, when Lord Kitchener came to see him, saying: "Well, there is one thing at any rate they cannot take from you. The Fleet was ready." But Churchill was still blamed for the losses at Gallipoli and was being ousted at a time when the campaign there was far from concluded. "I am finished," he said to a friend, "finished in respect of all I care for—the waging of war: the defeat of the Germans."

Although Churchill left the Admiralty on May 26, 1915, he was not immediately removed from all touch with the Dardanelles expedition. Asquith appointed him Chancellor of the Duchy of Lancaster, a post that carried more honor than responsibility. Churchill continued to be a member of the War Council, where he could present his strategic opinions. The council was divided in its views on the Dardanelles-Gallipoli situation, however, and many of its members considered that

Churchill's views were already discredited. The military situation deteriorated, and by fall there was growing discussion of the desirability of evacuating the troops from Gallipoli. Churchill found himself more and more out of harmony with the prevailing opinion. When it was decided to replace the War Council with a War Committee on which Churchill would not be included, he submitted his resignation from the government.

In a long farewell speech in the House of Commons on November 15, 1915, Churchill defended the part he had played in the Dardanelles operation, pointing out that at every stage it had been approved by the First Sea Lord and planned and executed by the navy. It was not, he said, "a civilian plan, foisted by a political amateur upon reluctant officers and experts." Despite the accuracy of his statements, his single-minded support of the operation was well known. Ill-deserved though it was, Churchill continued to be blamed for the failure.

Active Service in France

Although he was leaving the government, Churchill was determined to continue to do all that he could personally to participate in the fight against the Germans. He intended, he told the House of Commons, to enter "an alternative form of service to which no exception can be taken, and with which I am perfectly content." Four days later, as a major of the Oxfordshire Yeomanry, Churchill sailed to Boulogne. He was assigned first to a Grenadier Guards Battalion. There he was received with little warmth by officers who resented having a politician as a member of their mess. But his natural humor and courtesy, and his anxiety to learn and to participate once more in a soldier's life, soon broke through the resistance.

For the few weeks Churchill stayed with the Guards they remained in the trenches in the miserable Flanders weather of November and December. Although there was no major action, there was a constant exchange of fire with the Germans and a perpetual state of danger, discomfort, and misery in the trenches. As was always the case during his long life, when exposed to gunfire Churchill showed a complete lack of fear.

Sir John French offered Churchill command of a brigade, on the basis of his social and political prominence and his few years of experience as a professional soldier. But there was so much opposition to such an assignment in the House of Commons that Asquith forbade it. Instead, Churchill was promoted to lieutenant colonel and given command of the 6th Battalion of the Royal Scots Fusiliers. He joined his battalion near Armentières. Again he had to sell himself to officers and men who were not happy to be commanded by a politician—particularly one who had apparently failed because he had meddled in military affairs. He gained the confidence of his subordinates by conducting a successful campaign to rid them of lice.

In typical fashion, Churchill threw himself into the business of war. He kept his men busy improving their trenches. He worked them hard, almost as hard as he worked himself. Full of ideas, he tried them all out, not always with complete success. But the monotony of trench warfare began to wear on him. He knew that his talents were being wasted. He yearned to get back into the political arena, where he could have a greater influence on the conduct of the war.

Return to Parliament

The opportunity came during the early summer when Churchill's battalion was amalgamated with another, leaving him with no command. He wrote to the Secretary of State for War and requested release from the army to return to Parliament. His resignation was accepted, with the stipulation that he never again apply for military service.

At first Churchill's hopes for an active role in the prosecution of the war were frustrated. He found himself constantly under attack by his political enemies, and still unpopular with the public, which largely blamed him for the Gallipoli campaign and its bloody failure. His friends in the government could do nothing for him.

During the summer of 1916 the British army was engaged in the bloody and desperate offensive known to history as the Battle of the Somme. To Churchill the strategy of costly and fruitless assault of the German fortifications seemed very wrong. He continued to urge an attack in a weaker area. But he had no power in the government and his attempts to convince those who did were not successful.

Nor was he able to get support for his views on the use of the new tanks he had fostered. He pleaded that they should be

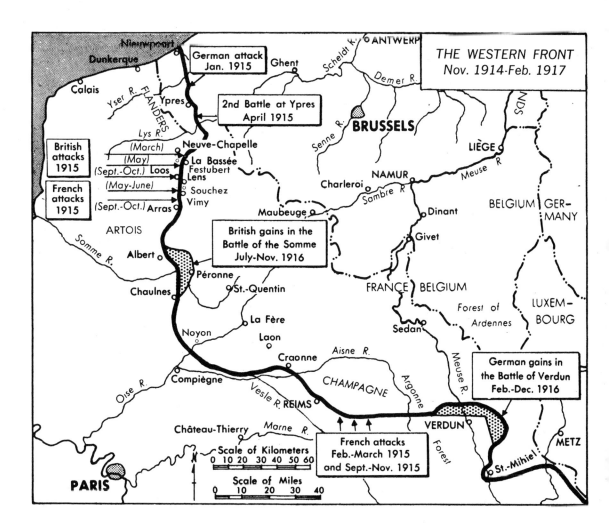

THE WESTERN FRONT
Nov. 1914-Feb. 1917

German attack
Jan. 1915

2nd Battle at Ypres
April 1915

British attacks 1915

French attacks 1915

(March)
(May)
(Sept.-Oct.) Loos
(May-June)
(Sept.-Oct.)

Neuve-Chapelle
La Bassée
Festubert
Lens
Souchez
Vimy
Arras

British gains in the
Battle of the Somme
July-Nov. 1916

German gains in
the Battle of Verdun
Feb.-Dec. 1916

French attacks
Feb.-March 1915
and Sept.-Nov. 1915

Nieuwpoort
Dunkerque
Calais
Ypres
FLANDERS
Yser R.
Lys R.
ARTOIS
Albert
Péronne
Chaulnes
St.-Quentin
La Fère
Noyon
Laon
Craonne
Compiègne
Somme R.
Oise R.
Maubeuge
Sedan
Château-Thierry
Marne R.
Vesle R. REIMS
Aisne R.
CHAMPAGNE
Argonne
Forest
VERDUN
METZ
St.-Mihiel
Meuse R.
PARIS

Ghent
ANTWERP
Scheldt R.
Demer R.
Senne R.
BRUSSELS
LIÈGE
Meuse R.
Charleroi
NAMUR
Sambre R.
Dinant
Givet
FRANCE BELGIUM
BELGIUM GER-MANY
NDS
Forest of
Ardennes
LUXEM-
BOURG

Scale of Kilometers
0 10 20 30 40 50 60

Scale of Miles
0 10 20 30 40

N

kept back until there were enough of them to be really effective; and he recommended more time to study their capabilities and limitations. But the tanks were used in small groups during the later stages of the Battle of the Somme. Although at first they startled the enemy, they accomplished little. This premature appearance removed all possibility of surprising the Germans later with an all-out armored attack.

In December, 1916, Asquith's government fell, to be replaced by a new coalition government headed by Churchill's friend David Lloyd George. Now, Churchill thought, he would certainly be given a chance to return to office. But his opponents in the government were too powerful. Lloyd George could not invite him to take a Cabinet post without jeopardizing bipartisan support.

In March, 1917, Lloyd George released the report of the Royal Commission which had investigated the Dardanelles operation. The report made it clear that any blame should at least be shared with Prime Minister Asquith and Lord Kitchener (who was now dead). Churchill's popularity in the House of Commons was somewhat increased in May when he delivered a long and fiery speech at a secret session. He attacked the unimaginative strategy of continuing the "squalid slaughter" of the trenches by attacks against the Germans' fortifications for the purpose of wearing them down and reducing their numbers. Britain and France should wait, he said, until the United States, which had just entered the war, could make her strength felt. Britain should concentrate on keeping the sea-lanes open and on combating the German U-boats.

The Minister of Munitions

By July of 1917 Lloyd George's position was so secure that he felt able to offer Churchill the post of Minister of Munitions. The appointment aroused strong opposition, and the government came close to a real crisis, but Lloyd George stood by his choice, and Churchill went to work.

As Minister of Munitions Churchill was not a member of the War Cabinet. However he was in a position to have some influence on the course of events. He reorganized the ministry and pushed production, greatly increasing the British supply of tanks, machine guns, and airplanes. He also provided the American Army with all of its medium artillery, lightening the load on American factories which were adapting their facilities from peace to war production.

Churchill took advantage of his new post to urge once more the proper use of tanks. He was exasperated by their misuse in 1916 and much of 1917. This misuse had made them very unpopular with most soldiers, who saw them attract much German artillery fire, but accomplish little. At last at Cambrai, in November, 1917, Sir Julian Byng achieved great success with a massed tank attack, following the general principles advocated by Churchill. No one was happier than he at this success.

During the rest of the war Churchill arranged his work so that he could spend a great deal of time near the front. He worked at the ministry in the morning and flew to France for the afternoon. He kept an office and sleeping quarters in a chateau close behind the lines. He was sleeping there when

Churchill was photographed standing by this World War I plane near the Western Front late in the war. (UPI)

Ludendorff launched the first of his great offensives against the British in March, 1918. As the defeated British troops retreated, a gap opened between them and the French. General Henri Pétain, the French Commander in Chief, refused to send reserves to help the British, because he expected the next German blow to be struck at Paris.

Churchill was not present at the top-level meetings of the British and French political and military leaders at Doullens on March 26 and at Beauvais on April 3. At the first of these, Field Marshal Sir Douglas Haig suggested that General Ferdinand Foch, the French Chief of Staff, be put in overall command of the Allied armies "from the Alps to the North Sea." But the actual agreement between cautious Prime Ministers Lloyd George and Clemenceau was merely to charge Foch "with the coordination of the action of the Allied Armies on the Western Front." The French and British commanders in chief were not under his command; they were merely "invited to furnish him with the necessary information."

On March 28, as the German armies continued to forge ahead, and with the gap between the British and French armies still unclosed, Lloyd George sent Churchill to Paris to find out what the French really intended to do. Would they help close the gap, and would they attack elsewhere on the front to take the pressure off the reeling British armies?

The immediate result of this delicate diplomatic mission was the establishment of a close and cordial relationship between Churchill and Premier Clemenceau. The old "Tiger" decided to go himself to the front with Churchill to observe the battle, to talk to the top commanders, and to find out just what was happening and what was planned.

Clemenceau's visits on March 29 and 30 to Foch, to Pétain, and to the principal British and French army commanders on

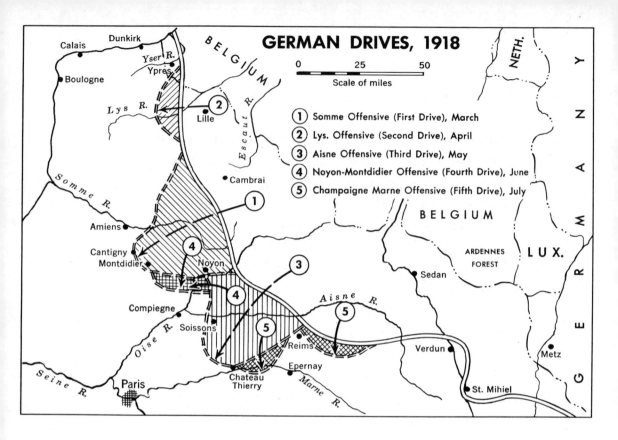

GERMAN DRIVES, 1918

Scale of miles
0   25   50

① Somme Offensive (First Drive), March
② Lys. Offensive (Second Drive), April
③ Aisne Offensive (Third Drive), May
④ Noyon-Montdidier Offensive (Fourth Drive), June
⑤ Champaigne Marne Offensive (Fifth Drive), July

either side of the German breakthrough seem to have convinced him of the need for more centralized authority. The visits certainly confirmed Churchill's own admiration for Foch's ability and determination. His confidential report of this whirlwind visit along the front must have been in Lloyd George's mind when the two prime ministers met at Beauvais on April 3 to appoint Foch the virtual Allied commander in chief, with full authority for the strategic direction of military operations on the Western Front.

There were four more German offensives in the spring and

early summer of 1918. In June, for a few hours, it seemed that the enemy might sweep across the Marne and into Paris. Churchill, concerned about the threat to factories producing materials for the Royal Air Force, rushed to Paris, where he was reassured by Clemenceau's stirring words: "I shall fight in front of Paris! I shall fight in Paris! I shall fight behind Paris!"

But the Germans were halted by French and American divisions at the Marne. It was their last serious threat. On July 18, just as Ludendorff's last offensive was grinding to a halt, Foch launched the first of a series of Allied counteroffensives. During the last four months of the war the Allies advanced slowly but steadily, wearing down the exhausted Germans, now dejected

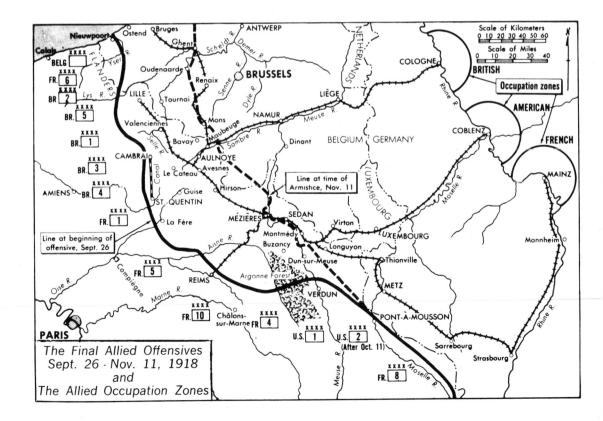

The Final Allied Offensives
Sept. 26 - Nov. 11, 1918
and
The Allied Occupation Zones

by their failure to achieve victory in their final, desperate offensives. By the beginning of November Germany's leaders recognized that they were completely defeated; the war ended when Germany virtually surrendered by accepting the Allies' severe Armistice terms on November 11, 1918.

Churchill, who spent more of these last months of the war in France than he did in London, was justly proud of the fact that part of the victory was due to the performance of Allied tanks. He was equally proud that an even more important part was played by the munitions production effort for which he was primarily responsible.

CHAPTER 6

A Voice in the Wilderness

Postwar Turmoil in Europe

The end of the war brought new problems. Churchill, as always, had strong views as to what should be done about them. Many Germans were near starvation, and to him it seemed more important to hold out a helping hand to rehabilitate a democratic Germany than to exact further punishment from the defeated. But public opinion was strongly opposed. When Lloyd George's government stood for elections in December, 1918, it was forced to adopt a policy of "Make the Germans Pay." By winning the election the government became committed to reparations, although many in the Cabinet, including Churchill, did not favor them.

In the re-elected government, Churchill became Secretary of State for War, with the Air Ministry included in his office. His first major problem was to demobilize the army. Demobilization had begun, but the system had been hastily prepared and was unfair to many men who had served since early in the war. There were mutinous rumblings throughout the army and a real mutiny in the Guards Brigade. Churchill not only straightened out the system, but he also succeeded in convincing both the public and the House of Commons that he was responsible for doing it. This did much to restore his popularity. His major concern, however, soon became the situation in Russia.

Following the overthrow of the Czar and the take-over of the central government by the Bolsheviks late in 1917, Russia had signed a separate peace with Germany in the spring of 1918. This had enabled Hindenburg and Ludendorff to move about a million men from the Eastern to the Western Front, providing the superiority of force that had almost won Ludendorff's spring offensives in 1918. To prevent the Germans from taking over Russian oil fields and stockpiles of munitions sent to Russia by the Allies, British troops had been sent into the Caucasus and to Archangel.

Now that the war was over, the British people thought these soldiers should return home. But a bitter civil war was raging in Russia, and the White Russians pleaded that the British troops should help them in their fight against the Bolsheviks.

Churchill was sympathetic to these pleas. "Of all the tyrannies in history," he said, "the Bolshevist tyranny is the worst, the most destructive, the most degrading. . . . The atrocities of Lenin and Trotsky are incomparably more hideous, on a larger scale, and more numerous than any for which the Kaiser is responsible. The Germans at any rate have stuck to their allies. They misled them, they exploited them, but they did not desert or betray them. It may have been honour among thieves, but it is better than dishonour among murderers."

Churchill could do nothing for the White Russians without

the approval of the Supreme Allied War Council, which was meeting in Paris. After three months of argument, in May, 1919, the Supreme Council took action. A note was sent to Admiral Aleksandr Kolchak, who commanded the White Russians in Siberia, telling him that the Allies did not wish to become involved in Russia's internal affairs, and so must soon withdraw the Allied troops. If, however, Kolchak would agree with the Allied policy of restoring "peace within Russia by enabling the Russian people to resume control of their own affairs through the agent of a freely elected Constituent Assembly," then the Allies would send munitions, supplies, and food.

With this authority, Churchill sent large quantities of ammunition and supplies into Russia. He was disappointed, however, to find that few people in Britain shared his suspicions of the Bolsheviks. Most considered this to be a Russian problem of no concern to Britain, and many were sympathetic with the new experiment in communism. Lloyd George refused to consider Churchill's arguments that Germany should be built up as a buffer against the spread of communism from Russia. Many Labour party spokesmen attacked Churchill vehemently. In the fall of 1919 the British troops were removed from Russia. White Russian resistance collapsed completely the following spring.

Early in 1920 war broke out between Poland and Russia. When the Red armies swept toward Moscow, Churchill feared that this was the beginning of a Bolshevik sweep into Central and Western Europe. Again he urged Lloyd George to build up Germany. But the Prime Minister took no action.

The Russian Civil War finally ended and the Poles repulsed

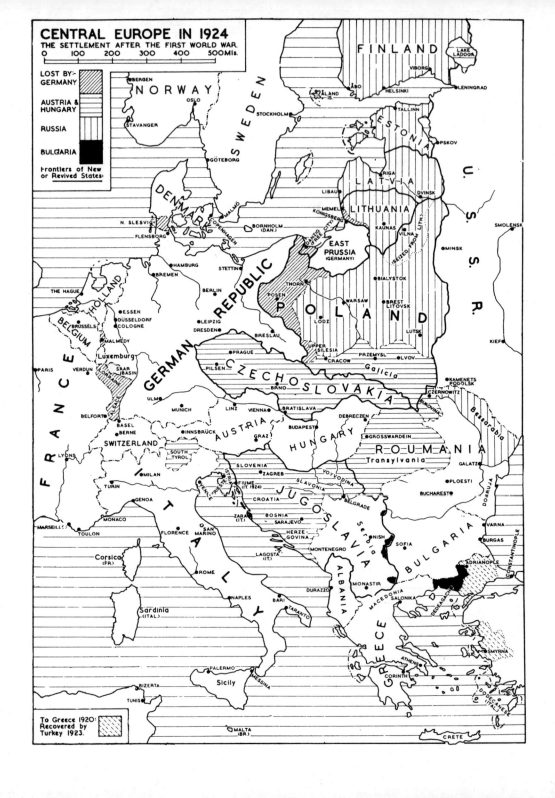

CENTRAL EUROPE IN 1924
THE SETTLEMENT AFTER THE FIRST WORLD WAR.

0   100   200   300   400   500 Mls.

LOST BY:-
GERMANY

AUSTRIA &
HUNGARY

RUSSIA

BULGARIA

Frontiers of New
or Revived States

To Greece 1920.
Recovered by
Turkey 1923.

the Russian invaders. But Churchill in January, 1921, still felt strongly. "What a monstrous absurdity and perversion of the truth it is, to represent the Communist theory as a form of progress, when, at every step and at every stage, it is simply marching back into the Dark Ages."

Nearer home, Ireland was in ferment. Churchill, who was now Colonial Secretary, was involved in the negotiations that eventually resulted in creation of the Irish Free State. He bore a large share of the responsibility of getting the agreement approved by Parliament.

Turmoil in the Middle East

As Colonial Secretary, Churchill also had to devote considerable attention to the Middle East. The Versailles Peace Conference, in disposing of former Turkish possessions, had given the French a mandate in Syria and the British mandates in Iraq and Palestine. The area seethed with discontent, and the British were forced to maintain 40,000 troops in Iraq to keep order. After a conference in Cairo, Churchill worked out a settlement that functioned effectively for many years. On the throne of Iraq he placed the Emir Faisal, the man who with the assistance of famed Thomas E. Lawrence "of Arabia"— had led the Arab revolt against the Turks during the war. This settled a dispute between France and the Arabs, who had hoped to control Syria at the end of the war. Churchill also worked out an adjustment between Arabs and Jews in Palestine.

Britain had meanwhile become indirectly involved in a war that had broken out between Turkey and Greece. For political reasons, France and Italy refused to join Britain in maintaining the postwar settlements for Turkey. They withdrew their troops from the straits region when Mustafa Kemal Pasha, head of a new Turkish republic, threatened to take back by force Turkey's prewar possessions in Europe. This left the British alone guarding the Dardanelles with a contingent at Chanak, as a Turkish army approached.

In a blunt communiqué, undoubtedly written by Churchill, Britain called on the British Dominions and the Balkan states to help to prevent the Turks from crossing the strait into Europe. Faced by the Royal Navy and a well-prepared British ground contingent, Mustafa Kemal withdrew his troops and shortly thereafter—October 10, 1922—signed an armistice. But the British people were upset that the government had taken measures which might well have led Britain into war. Popular protests helped to bring down the coalition government of Lloyd George.

Electoral Defeat

For the first time since 1900 Churchill was defeated in the election that followed, and late in 1922 found himself no longer a member of the House of Commons. To occupy himself he turned to writing and to his hobby of painting. In 1923 he produced his own story of World War I, *The World Crisis*. It was criticized by many, with some justification, as being not history but autobiography. It was indeed written with a strong bias, and it includes his own version of the Dardanelles affair, in which his part is stoutly defended. But as source material for the history of the period the five volumes are invaluable. While the documentation is obviously selected to support his case, the evidence is impressive as well as authentic.

The World Crisis includes a penetrating analysis of the causes of World War I and discussions of the quantitative factors of the war which foreshadowed later development of the art of operations research. Churchill's review and analysis of the casualties on both sides of the Western Front were a major contribution to the study of the real significance of the action there. *The World Crisis* is, at the same time, a work of real literary merit. It proved very popular, and with his profits from it Churchill bought a country house, Chartwell Manor.

Churchill's political future at this time seemed bleak. The Liberal party, of which he was a member, had done so poorly in the election that its place as the opposition party had been taken over by Labour. He and the Labourites held mutual feelings of dislike. And the Conservatives, considering him a traitor, would have no part of him.

In 1923 another general election was held, and again Churchill met defeat. He failed still again the following year in a contest for a seat in the Abbey Division of Westminster. However, in that election he had campaigned as an independent candidate and had built up a considerable amount of Conservative support.

In the fall Churchill ran in Epping in another general election, this time as a Constitutionalist with Conservative support. He was elected, and the Conservative Prime Minister, Stanley Baldwin, promptly appointed him Chancellor of the Exchequer.

Although finances were not a primary interest of Winston Churchill, he had long aspired to be Chancellor of the Exchequer, the second most important Cabinet post. This was a period of financial crisis and economic unrest in England and Churchill lacked the economic training and financial experience which the post required in such difficult times. Nevertheless he remained in the office as long as the Baldwin government continued in power. When the Labour party won the general election of 1929, Churchill, together with the other Conservatives, left the government. It was ten years before he returned.

Churchill remained in Parliament during those years, however, and he continued to write. Having finished the fifth volume of *The World Crisis*—"The Aftermath"—in 1929, he went to work on a history of the sector of the war in which he had not participated, the Eastern Front. This book, published in 1931 with the title, *The Unknown War*, was not as thorough as most of his historical works, but it could hardly be criticized, for nothing else of value on the Eastern Front had been published in English. (Later the book was published as Volume VI of *The World Crisis*.)

Next Churchill plunged into research for a biography of his most famous ancestor, John Churchill, the first Duke of Marlborough. This intense study of the art of war and of a period of crisis parallel to that of World War II was to prove of great value to him when he led his nation from 1940 to 1945.

The Loner

Politically, Churchill had already become unpopular with the Conservatives when the Cabinet fell in 1929; in following years he drifted farther from the views of the Conservative leader, Stanley Baldwin. Churchill's place in the leadership of the Conservative party ended when he refused to join in supporting a federal government and dominion status for India. A staunch defender of the British Empire, he remained opposed to relaxing control over India to the end. In the succeeding years he became more and more of a loner, championing the causes in which he believed, regardless of the political implications.

During these postwar years popular sentiment in Britain was strong for pacifism and disarmament. Churchill was almost alone in recognizing the nature of the upheaval going on in Germany during the rise of the Nazi party. In impassioned speeches he urged the strengthening of Britain's defenses and a strong stand against Hitler and the growing power of Germany. Although he was out of the government and had no access to official reports, he developed his own sources of intelligence and closely watched the moves being made on the Continent. When Germany demanded the right to rearm in the summer of 1932, Churchill warned the House of Commons:

. . . Do not let His Majesty's Government believe that all that Germany is asking for is equal status. . . . All these bands of sturdy Teutonic youths, marching through the streets and roads of Germany, with the light of desire in their eyes to suffer for the Fatherland, are not looking for status. They are looking for weapons, and, when they have the weapons, believe me they will then ask for the return of their lost territories and lost colonies, and when the demand is made it cannot fail to shake and possibly shatter [many countries] to their foundations. . . . The removal of the just grievances of the vanquished ought to precede the disarmament of the victors. To bring about anything like equality of armaments [between the vanquished and the victor nations] if it were in our power to do so, which it happily is not, while those grievances remain unredressed, would be almost to appoint the day for another European war—to fix it as though it were a prize fight.

Two months later Hitler came into power in Germany, yet the British government, then led by Ramsay MacDonald, continued to urge the French to disarm. "Thank God for the French Army," said Churchill. "At a moment like this, to ask France to halve her army while Germany doubles hers, to ask France to halve her air force while the German air force remains whatever it is, is a proposal likely to be considered by the French Government, at present at any rate, as somewhat unseasonable." The House scoffed, but the French refused to cut their army.

Unheeded Warnings

The Versailles Treaty at the end of World War I had forbidden Germany to develop an air force, but she evaded this prohibition by organizing a network of glider clubs that could readily be converted to a military air force. When Churchill warned the House of Commons what was going on, his words went unheeded. In November, 1934, he spoke out again:

I assert, first, that Germany already, at this moment, has a military air force—that is to say, military squadrons, with the necessary ground services, and the necessary reserves of trained personnel and material—which only awaits an order to assemble in full open combination; and that this illegal air force is rapidly approaching equality with our own. Secondly, by this time next year, if Germany executes her existing programme without acceleration, and if we execute our existing programme on the basis which now lies before us without slowing down, and carry out the increases announced to Parliament in July last, the German military air force will this time next year be in fact at least as strong as our own, and it may be even stronger. Thirdly, on the same basis—that is to say, both sides continuing with their existing programmes as at present arranged—by the end of 1936, that is, one year farther on, and two years from now—the German military air force will be nearly fifty per cent stronger, and in 1937 nearly double. All this is on the assumption, as I say, that there is no acceleration on the part of Germany, and no slowing-down on our part.

Not so, said Stanley Baldwin, who once again was acting Prime Minister.* Germany's "real strength is not fifty per cent of our strength in Europe today," he said. "As for the position this time next year . . . we estimate that we shall still have a margin in Europe alone of nearly fifty per cent." The members of the House were reassured.

Four months later, however, in March, 1935, Germany announced that the German air force was equal in strength to the British. When Baldwin acknowledged this, admitting he had been in error before, he was acclaimed for his honesty and soon afterward won a general election with a great majority. Churchill remained in the House of Commons, but he was still unpopular with the people and with his fellow members. Instead of being given credit, most people resented the fact that he had been right, as though he and not Hitler had been responsible for deceiving the inept British Prime Minister. Although the position of First Lord of the Admiralty was available, Baldwin refused to include Churchill in his new government. Few Conservatives supported him, and many believed—even hoped —that his political career was over.

By 1936 Churchill was urging the strengthening of the League of Nations to unite the nations of Europe against Hitler, but Baldwin remained unconvinced. When Hitler occupied the Rhineland in March, France refused to move without British support and Baldwin would not give it outside the League.

* Ramsay MacDonald was nominally Prime Minister of a coalition government, but the Conservatives had a majority in the House of Commons, and Baldwin really controlled the government.

Winston Churchill in 1937. (National Archives)

Nevertheless, the evidence of German rearmament was now slowly beginning to swing popular opinion to agree with Churchill. He continued to call for stronger defenses and for the nations to unite against the German threat.

Churchill's growing popularity was soon wiped out, however, in the Abdication Crisis. In this most difficult time, Churchill was almost the only public figure who stood by King Edward VIII in the face of clamor from all sides for his abdication. Churchill urged the government to move slowly, to allow time to work out a solution. But the king was forced to abdicate at once, and Churchill was bitterly accused not only of bad judgment but of trying to wreck the British Constitution. Again he found himself virtually ignored by his fellow Conservatives.

Although Baldwin did not ask Churchill to serve in the Cabinet, he was given a place on a new Committee of Air Defence Research. Minor though his influence could be in such a post, Churchill made it his business to learn all he could about air defense, and he also took advantage of free access to the Admiralty to keep aware of what was going on there. By 1939 he knew a great deal about the latest developments in the two most vital areas for defense of Britain.

On May 28, 1937, Baldwin resigned, to be replaced as Prime Minister by Neville Chamberlain. Although Churchill supported Chamberlain's appointment, he opposed his policy consistently. For where Churchill wanted arms and a coalition to resist Hitler, Chamberlain believed he could control Hitler with diplomacy and appeasement. Churchill's warnings continued to be almost entirely unheeded. In March, 1938, two weeks after Hitler moved into Austria, Churchill spoke in the House of Commons:

> Now the victors are vanquished, and those who threw down their arms in the field and sued for an armistice are striding on to world mastery. That is the position—that is the terrible transformation that has taken place bit by bit. I rejoice to hear from the Prime Minister that a further supreme effort is to be made to place us in a position of security. Now is the time at last to rouse the nation. Perhaps it is the last time it can be roused with a chance of preventing war, or with a chance of coming through to victory should our efforts to prevent war fail. We should lay aside every hindrance and endeavour by uniting the whole force and spirit of our people to raise again a great British nation standing up before all the world; for such a nation, rising in its ancient vigour, can even at this hour save civilization.

His oratory was greeted with silence. His warnings were still ignored.

Munich

"Peace in our time," was Chamberlain's objective, and when it appeared that the Munich Conference of September, 1938, had prevented war, he was proclaimed a hero. Most Britons agreed with him when he spoke of German claims against Czechoslovakia as being of no concern to Britain: ". . . a quarrel in a far-away country between people of whom we know nothing!"

Few agreed with Churchill when he said, "Many people, no doubt, honestly believe that they are only giving away the interest of Czechoslovakia, whereas I fear we shall find that we have deeply compromised, and perhaps fatally endangered, the safety and even the independence of Great Britain and France. . . . There can never be friendship between the British democracy and the Nazi power, that power which spurns Christian ethics, which cheers its onward course by barbarous paganism, which vaunts the spirit of aggression and conquest, which derives strength and perverted pleasure from persecution, and uses, as we have seen, with pitiless brutality the threat of murderous force. That power cannot ever be the trusted friend of British democracy. . . . This is only the first sip, the first foretaste of the bitter cup which will be proffered to us year by year, unless by a supreme recovery of moral health and martial vigour, we arise again and take our stand for freedom as in the olden time."

Churchill's characterization of Munich as "a disaster of the first magnitude" met with strong protests. Hope blinded the eyes of the majority, not only in Britain but throughout the

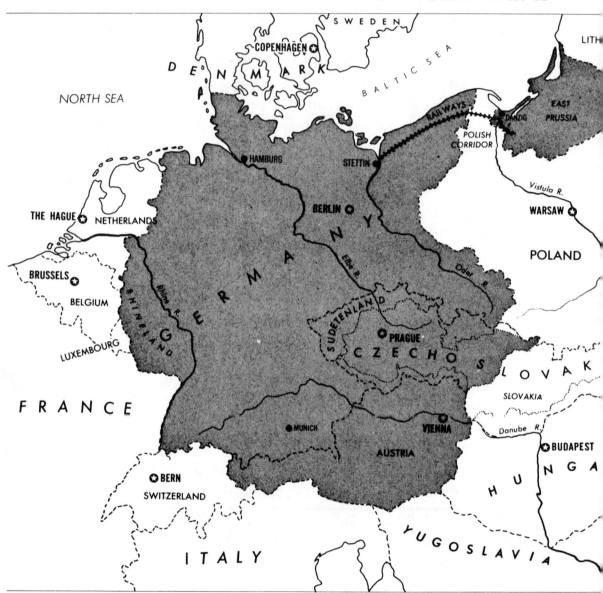

world. Still, Churchill had the courage to face up to the facts and to proclaim them as he saw them, although few listened and many scorned.

Six months later, when Hitler's soldiers marched into Prague, Chamberlain and the world realized that appeasement was of no use. By then the firm stand for which Churchill had been calling for for five years had to be made on the indefensible frontiers of Poland.

CHAPTER 7

"Winston Is Back"

Return to the Admiralty

In the early morning hours of September 1, 1939, German armies invaded Poland. Chamberlain at last faced up to reality and to Britain's treaty obligations to Poland. After declaration of war against Germany, at 11:00 A.M. on September 3, he offered Churchill the post of First Lord of the Admiralty. Nothing could have pleased Churchill more than to return to the seat he had left so unpleasantly in 1915 and to hold again in his hands the controls of the Royal Navy. Eager to get to work at once, he was at his desk by six o'clock the same afternoon. A signal had already gone from the Admiralty to all the fleet— "Winston is back!"

During the years between the wars Churchill had been keeping abreast of naval affairs and he knew a great deal about the fleet he would have to work with and the job it would have to do. There was no likelihood of great naval engagements, for the German navy was too small to challenge the British on the surface.

U-boats were another story. As Churchill was taking over in

the Admiralty on September 3 they claimed their first victim, the passenger liner *Athenia*. Churchill at once ordered the convoy system and other antisubmarine measures to be put in effect in accordance with prewar doctrine. Protection of the fleet from the U-boats and from air attacks was a more difficult problem and one to which Churchill devoted immediate attention, calling for all possible measures of concealment and defense. In the north, between Scotland and Iceland, a blockade was set up like the one maintained during World War I, to halt merchant shipping on the way to German ports.

Although Churchill was responsible for the navy, in his capacity as a member of the War Cabinet he was soon sending memoranda in all directions. As in World War I, he offered his suggestions and advice in areas not directly in his area of responsibility. In mid-September he predicted that Hitler would not attack in the West until his situation was secure in the East. Nevertheless, Churchill urged, the French-Belgian frontier should be fortified and heavily protected against tank attack. To the Chancellor of the Exchequer he recommended a campaign against waste, even to the reuse of envelopes. On the first day of October he was recommending replacing the professional troops in India with others with less training and using the men from India as cadres for training eight or ten field divisions in southern France.

Early in September Churchill started to try to do something about a problem he remembered from World War I. Germany was dependent upon Sweden for much of her supply of iron ore. During the summer months, as long as Sweden remained

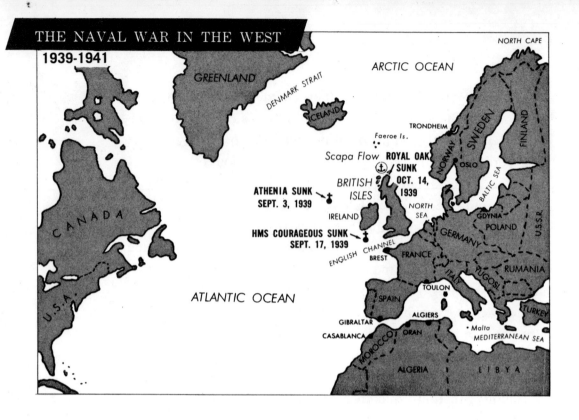

neutral, there was little that Britain could do to interfere with the shipment of ore across the Baltic Sea. But in the winter Sweden's northeastern ports would be frozen, and the shipments could be expected to travel, as they had in World War I, across Norway to the northern port of Narvik, and then down the Norwegian coast to Germany. As long as the ships kept within Norway's territorial waters, under international law the British fleet could not interfere with them. Churchill urged that arrangements be sought with Norway to mine this passageway. As part of the scheme he recommended that Britain should try to charter Norwegian ships and buy up Swedish iron ore, so that

96

the two Scandinavian countries would not suffer from loss of trade with Germany. Churchill convinced the War Cabinet that his idea was good, but could not get any agreement to take action.

At the end of November, Russia attacked Finland. The sympathy of the Allied peoples was with the Finns, and means were sought to aid them. The shortest route, and the only one available in the winter, was through Narvik and then by railroad across Norway and Sweden. But in February, Sweden turned down the Allied request for passage. Meanwhile, the Germans had been developing other plans.

In early October, Admiral Erich Raeder, Chief of the German Naval Staff, persuaded Hitler that Germany would profit by controlling bases in Norway and denying the Scandinavian countries to the British. Hitler at once ordered plans for the occupation of Norway and development of a supporting "fifth column" inside the country.

The Struggle for Norway

Finland accepted Russian armistice terms on March 20, 1940, removing an excuse for the British to use Narvik and control the railroad. But the desirability of mining the passageway along the Norwegian west coast remained. The Cabinet finally agreed that, despite Norway's neutrality, the operation should begin on April 8, 1940. In the early dawn of that morning four destroyers laid a minefield just off the entrance to the port of Narvik, and a note was handed to the Norwegian Foreign Minister to explain the action.

Meanwhile German forces were already heading for Norwegian ports. At dawn on April 9, German troops landed at points all along the coast of Norway. The British naval forces taking part in the mine-laying operation were soon engaging German vessels with considerable success. But there was no prospect of dislodging the German troops on the shores. A pro-Nazi organization headed by Vidkun Quisling declared itself the government of Norway, and the carefully developed fifth column helped German troops drive the legal government out of Oslo.

The Norwegians, resisting the German invasion with all their resources, called on Britain and France for help. An operation to retake all of Norway was out of the question, for the troops could not be spared from France. But attacks were planned on two main ports, Narvik and Trondheim. Churchill favored Narvik and would have preferred to concentrate on that alone. But he went along with the decision of the War Cabinet to try to take Trondheim. By this time, however, German reinforcements were pouring into Norway by air. The Allied operation, "too little and too late," was unsuccessful, and the troops were evacuated. At Narvik, however, the British drove the Germans out and held the city by May 28. Within a few days, however, the British forces were removed for urgent use in Holland, Belgium, and France.

The setbacks in Norway, including the loss of several British ships in the engagements off the Norwegian coast, had led the House of Commons to call for a debate on the issue on May 9. Chamberlain's government received a bare majority vote. The following day German troops poured across the borders into Holland and Belgium. It was clear to the Prime Minister that in this crisis there must be a coalition government, to ensure support of all political parties for the hard days that lay ahead. He thereupon decided to resign. At his recommendation, the king summoned Churchill and asked him to form a new government.

CHAPTER 8

The Finest Hour

Disaster in Flanders

At last Churchill had achieved the position of top responsibility in Britain, and at a time when strong, brilliant, imaginative leadership was essential. To ensure a firm grasp on that responsibility, he reorganized the government. In addition to his post as Prime Minister he assumed the duties of Minister of Defence. This was a new office, coordinating the Admiralty, the War Office, and the Air Ministry.

Churchill did not ask Parliament for special powers, nor did he define the duties of the Minister of Defence. He merely assumed responsibility for general direction of the war, through supervision and direction of the Chiefs of Staff Committee—the senior officers of each of the three services. For the first time in British history, the nation's military leaders exercised their responsibility for strategic planning and day-to-day operations under the direct supervision of the head of the government. At various times in the coming months and years Churchill assumed other powers, on a temporary basis, assuring him full control of the war effort and making him a virtual dictator.

Three days after becoming Prime Minister, Churchill called for a vote of confidence in the House of Commons. In a brief and stirring speech that has become a classic in English literature, he told the members that he could offer them nothing "but blood, toil, tears and sweat." His policy, he said, was to wage war; his aim was victory. "Come, then," he said, "let us go forward together with our united strength." The vote of support was unanimous, as members of all parties fell into line behind him.

Meanwhile, German ground troops and tanks had seized Luxembourg and were pouring into Belgium, Holland, and northern France. On May 13, after a surprise blow through the Ardennes, they smashed their way across the Meuse and through hastily formed French defenses as Sedan and Mézières. Their spearhead dashed westward toward the Channel.

During the disastrous days that followed, Churchill took an active part in trying to avert total catastrophe. He flew to France to confer with French leaders and made numerous suggestions of tactical measures to be taken. Most of these were ignored, and the inexorable German drive toward the Channel coast continued.

It was obvious to Churchill that the threat to the Allies was even greater than during Ludendorff's first offensive in 1918. Remembering the importance of American assistance in those dark days, Churchill again turned to the United States for support. On May 15 he sent President Roosevelt a message, asking for the loan of destroyers to help fight the U-boats, and also for aircraft, artillery, antiaircraft equipment and ammuni-

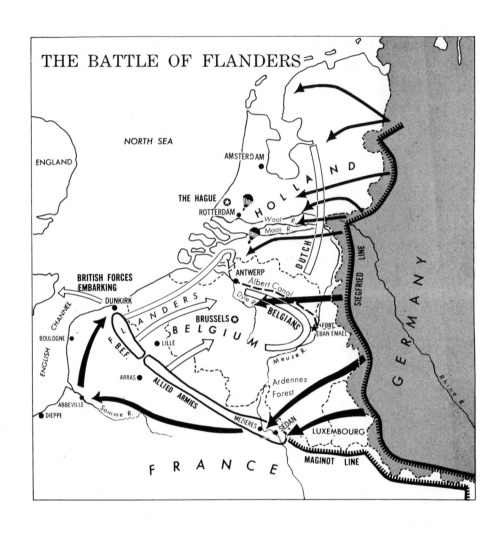

THE BATTLE OF FLANDERS

ENGLAND

NORTH SEA

AMSTERDAM

THE HAGUE
ROTTERDAM

HOLLAND

Waal R.
Maas R.

DUTCH

SIEGFRIED LINE

GERMANY

Rhine R.

BRITISH FORCES
EMBARKING

DUNKIRK

ANTWERP
Albert Canal

FLANDERS

BRUSSELS

BELGIANS

BELGIUM

FORT
EBAN EMAEL

ENGLISH CHANNEL

BOULOGNE

B.E.F.

LILLE

Meuse R.

ARRAS

ALLIED ARMIES

Ardennes
Forest

ABBEVILLE
DIEPPE

Somme R.

MEZIERES

SEDAN

LUXEMBOURG

FRANCE

MAGINOT LINE

tion, and steel. Five days later he painted a blunt picture of the future if the United States should leave Britain and France to their fate. Roosevelt at once took measures to provide most of these things, but he did not yet see a way to send the destroyers Churchill badly needed, since he knew that the American people were not yet ready to enter the war.

On May 20, as the German armored columns approached the coast near Abbeville, it was clear that most of the BEF and nearly half of the French army would be cut off in Belgium and French Flanders. Foreseeing the possibility that the troops north of the breakthrough area might be driven to the coast, Churchill ordered the Admiralty to "assemble a large number of small vessels in readiness to proceed to ports and inlets on the French Coast."

Dunkirk

As Churchill feared, the BEF was driven back toward the sea, concentrating in a pocket around the port of Dunkirk. Churchill followed this action closely and made constant comments and recommendations for action to the War Office. Sadly he decided that a smaller force in Calais should not be relieved, but must fight on to keep as much as possible of the weight of the German attack away from the larger force which he now was determined to try to evacuate.

Starting on the evening of May 26, the British soldiers of the Expeditionary Force, and a large part of the French First

Army, were taken from the beaches around Dunkirk back to Britain. In an operation that had been partly planned at Churchill's urgent demand, and that partly developed to fill the need, virtually every vessel on the south coast of England—yachts, tugs, fishing boats, lifeboats—joined the naval craft that were heading for Dunkirk. In all, some 850 vessels participated in the operation, safely removing over 300,000 men from the beaches, despite repeated German air attacks. But the air threat dwindled as hundreds of German planes were shot down in fierce counterattacks by the fighter planes of the Royal Air Force.

As the evacuation began, and the fall of France appeared increasingly imminent, Churchill requested the considered view of the Chiefs of Staff Committee on "the prospects of . . . continuing the war alone against Germany and probably Italy." Weighing the situation carefully, the military chiefs replied: ". . . our conclusion is that *prima facie* Germany has most of the cards; but the real test is whether the morale of our fighting personnel and civil population will counterbalance the numerical and material advantages which Germany enjoys. We believe it will."

"We Shall Never Surrender"

Morale was the key, and Churchill was the man who could best maintain it in the fiber of the British people. In strict confidence he called on his colleagues in the government to maintain high morale in their areas and to show "confidence in our ability and inflexible resolve to continue the war till we have broken the will of the enemy to bring all Europe under his domination."

Churchill had the wholehearted support of his Cabinet Ministers in his determination to fight on. When, on June 4, he reported to the Parliament, he roused the feelings of that body, of all the people of Britain, and indeed of the free world, with the immortal words:

Even though large tracts of Europe and many old and famous States have fallen or may fall into the grip of the Gestapo and all the odious apparatus of Nazi rule, we shall not flag or fail. We shall go on to the end, we shall fight in France, we shall fight in the seas and oceans, we shall fight with growing confidence and growing strength in the air, we shall defend our island, whatever the cost may be, we shall fight on the beaches, we shall fight on the landing-grounds, we shall fight in the fields and in the streets, we shall fight in the hills; we shall never surrender, and even if, which I do not for a moment believe, this island or a large part of it were subjugated and starving, then our Empire beyond the seas, armed and guarded by the British Fleet, would carry on the struggle, until, in God's good time, the New World, with all its power and might, steps forth to the rescue and the liberation of the Old.

Italy had remained neutral during the first months of the war. Churchill tried in vain to persuade Mussolini at least to

Churchill flashes his famous "V for Victory" sign during the darkest days of the war. (UPI)

106

remain on the sidelines. His overtures were rebuffed, and Mussolini clearly indicated that he was going to join Germany. Churchill sent a stream of memoranda to the service chiefs, recommending measures to be taken in preparation for Mussolini's declaration of war. When it came, on June 10, 1940, British forces at Gibraltar promptly seized five Italian ships that were anchored there, and British bombers flew at once from England to bomb the Italian cities of Turin and Milan.

As soon as the evacuees from Dunkirk could be reassembled and refitted in England, two divisions were hurried back to France. With a third that had remained in France they tried to make a stand against the onrushing Germans. But there were only about 65 discouraged Allied divisions to face 124 divisions of well-trained, well-armed, enthusiastic Germans. Within a few days the Allies were being pushed back all along the line, and one British division had been cut off.

The Collapse of France

During this critical period Churchill conferred frequently with the French leaders, making four flights to France to talk with Premier Reynaud, who was shifting his government to Bordeaux. Churchill—remembering Clemenceau's determination in 1918—pleaded with the French to defend Paris street by street if necessary. This was not an appealing idea to men who had already decided that surrender was the only feasible

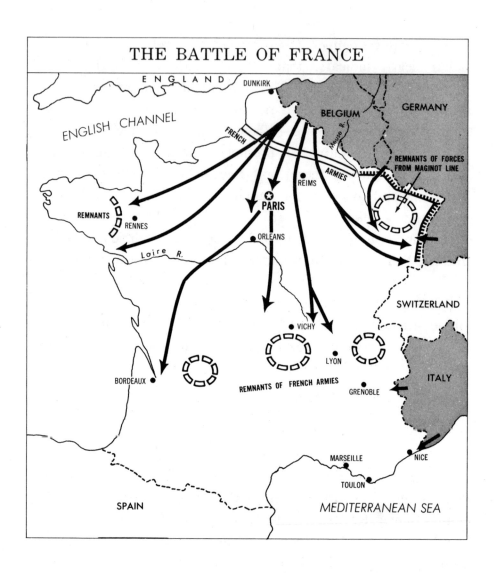

THE BATTLE OF FRANCE

ENGLAND

DUNKIRK

ENGLISH CHANNEL

BELGIUM

GERMANY

FRENCH

Meuse R.

ARMIES

REMNANTS OF FORCES
FROM MAGINOT LINE

REIMS

★ PARIS

REMNANTS

RENNES

ORLEANS

Loire R.

SWITZERLAND

VICHY

LYON

BORDEAUX

REMNANTS OF FRENCH ARMIES

ITALY

GRENOBLE

MARSEILLE

NICE

TOULON

SPAIN

MEDITERRANEAN SEA

course. This group won out over those other Frenchmen who were determined not to yield.

Finally, as the Germans were pouring through Paris, the French Cabinet asked the British for permission to request terms for an armistice. The Allies had an agreement not to make separate terms with the enemy. Churchill knew that the French would surrender whether he agreed or not. So he reluctantly agreed, but on condition that the ships of the French fleet, then fourth in size in the world, be delivered to British ports. Unfortunately, this condition, which would have removed the menace of these vessels to the Royal Navy, was not fulfilled.

On June 17, Reynaud resigned as Premier, to be replaced by the aging Marshal Pétain. Twenty-two years earlier, Churchill had noted and forthrightly recorded in *The World Crisis*, Pétain's defeatism in the face of Ludendorff's first offensive. The years had not made the old marshal any more determined. He promptly requested an armistice and ordered all French forces to stop fighting. The British forces, which had been fighting in the north, made their way as rapidly as they could to Cherbourg, where 156,000 men, including about 20,000 Polish troops, were evacuated before the Germans could reach the port.

The ships of the French fleet were scattered in several ports of the Mediterranean, including the main British base at Alexandria. A few were in English ports. The armistice terms, which Pétain's government accepted from Germany, provided that all French warships should be assembled in French ports, to be demobilized and disarmed under German or Italian direction. But Churchill had little faith in Hitler's promises and feared that the Germans would take over these ships and use them against Britain. So he obtained approval of his Cabinet to seize, control, or if necessary disable or destroy them.

On July 3, British boarding parties seized the French ships that lay at Portsmouth and Plymouth. The French admiral in Alexandria, threatened by the guns of the British Mediterranean Fleet, agreed to discharge the oil from his ships so that they could not move and to remove parts of the mechanisms of their guns so that they could not fire. In Martinique, after prolonged negotiations, the French ships were immobilized under an agreement with the United States.

The largest French squadron, including the modern battle cruisers *Dunkerque* and *Strasbourg*, was at Oran. A British squadron, under Vice Admiral Sir James Somerville, arrived off that port on July 3 and presented the French admiral with an ultimatum to yield his ships, intern them, or sink them. The French admiral refused. Under orders from the War Cabinet, Somerville opened fire. A fierce fight followed. The *Dunkerque* ran aground, one French battleship blew up, and another was beached. But the *Strasbourg* escaped and fled safely to Toulon.

When the battleship *Richelieu* was effectively disabled in the harbor of Dakar there was little left of the French navy for the Germans to put to use. Despite the unpleasant aspects of such use of force against recent friends and allies, this show of resolution not only strengthened the position of the British fleet but demonstrated to the world the determination and the sincerity in Churchill's words of confidence.

Britain Stands Alone

Following the German victory in France, the world expected an early German assault across the English Channel. Churchill set in motion a wide variety of measures for defense of the island against sea and air attack. No phase of the defense program was too small or too complex for his attention, whether it was in the organization of the Home Guard of civilians or the development of a magnetic bomb that would stick to German tanks as they moved up the beaches. He called on all Britons to help prepare the defenses, and they echoed his determination never to surrender.

By August of 1940 obstacles had been built on the beaches and around major installations. Antiaircraft guns were installed, and the heaviest guns available had been mounted on the southern coast at Churchill's insistence, pointing across the Channel toward France. When German guns on the French coast opened fire on convoys passing through the Channel toward Dover and London, the British guns were ready to reply. Guns and ammunition were also beginning to arrive from the United States to be put into the hands of soldiers and civilians for Britain's defense.

With confidence in Britain's overwhelming naval superiority

and in the efficiency of the Royal Air Force against large odds, Churchill foresaw little likelihood of a successful German attempt to invade Britain. Even when intelligence sources reported in August that Hitler had ordered an attack on the south coast of England, Operation "Sea Lion," Churchill was confident that the Germans did not have the facilities to make a successful invasion. But he insisted on every possible measure to prevent or delay a landing from the sea, and was particularly concerned that the army be located strategically to repel an invasion wherever it might come.

The island waited. In the words of Churchill, "Far out on the grey waters of the North Sea and the Channel coursed and patrolled the faithful, eager flotillas peering through the night. High in the air soared the fighter pilots, or waited serene at a moment's notice around their excellent machines."

It was the air which was the question mark in 1940. As Churchill well knew, "the passage of an army across salt water in the face of superior fleets and flotillas is an almost impossible feat." But what if the enemy controlled the air over the sea? Best intelligence figures showed the German air strength at three to one over the British. But Churchill "rested upon the conclusion that in our own air, over our own country and its waters, we could beat the German Air Force. And if this were true, our naval power would continue to rule the seas and oceans, and would destroy all enemies who set their course towards us."

It was obvious to both sides that the first step for a German invasion must be the destruction of England's air power. "The question was," wrote Churchill later, "how this would end between the combatants; and in addition the Germans wondered whether the British people would stand up to the air bombardment, the effect of which in these days was greatly exaggerated, or whether they would crumple and force His Majesty's Government to capitulate. About this Reichmarshal Goering had high hopes, and we had no fears."

The all-out air attack on Britain began on July 10, 1940, and lasted until the end of September. The British people withstood the suffering and disaster the bombs inflicted, constantly encouraged by Churchill, who shared the danger and the sorrow. He repeatedly visited the bombed-out areas, where his appearance unfailingly encouraged and cheered the people. The Royal Air Force was strained to the very limit of its endurance and capabilities, but plane losses were nearly two to one in favor of the British.

When this Battle of Britain failed to knock out the Royal Air Force, Goering turned from daylight to night bombing and to mass attacks on British cities. The British withstood the bombings and the destruction of this "blitz" until May, 1941, when the German bombing was halted. It had failed to bring about the surrender Hitler had expected and had resulted in the destruction of large numbers of German planes and the loss of hundreds of Germany's best pilots.

The invasion never came. Churchill's confident strategic assessment was confirmed.

Shown here amid the ruins of a bombing raid on London in 1941, Churchill symbolized the resolute determination of Great Britain when she stood
alone against the military might of Germany. (UPI)

While the British were bending all their efforts to stay alive, Churchill was already urging his military subordinates to begin offensive operations in whatever ways were possible. A return to the continent of Europe in force would be unthinkable for some time but, he said, small raiding parties could be put ashore to do specific jobs and then withdraw. They could keep sizable numbers of German troops pinned down along the coast of the occupied countries and unable to participate in an attack on Britain. Organization of the raiding forces known as Commandos began at once. They were to make a record of which all Britons could be proud.

Plans for a future offensive on a larger scale gave Churchill an opportunity to try out some ideas he had developed in earlier years. One was for craft to support amphibious landings by carrying tanks and putting them ashore ahead of or with the infantry. Another was for the creation of artificial harbors on unprotected shores by towing vessels made of concrete to the area and sinking them off the beach. It would be several years before this idea could be tried, but construction proceeded at once on LCT's (Landing Craft, Tank), and the larger LST's (Landing Ship, Tank), as well as on many smaller craft.

During the long summer of 1940 Churchill renewed his plea to President Roosevelt for help, and particularly for the loan or gift of fifty old destroyers that had recently been reconditioned in the United States. A scheme was finally worked out within

Roosevelt's constitutional authority, and in September final arrangements were made for the exchange of the destroyers in return for ninety-nine-year leases to the United States of naval and air bases in British possessions in the Western Hemisphere.

Italy's declaration of war and the collapse of France opened a new area where British land forces were in contact with the enemy: North Africa. The British had about 50,000 men assigned to the defense of their bases in Egypt and, more importantly, to defense of the Suez Canal and access to the Eastern Mediterranean. West of Egypt were the Italian colonies of Cyrenaica and Tripolitania (parts of Libya), and to the south, large Italian garrisons were stationed in Ethiopia, Eritrea, and Somaliland. From the main Italian base at Tripoli a new road led along the coast to the Egyptian frontier, where about 70,000 to 80,000 Italian troops were reported assembled.

Churchill, realizing that an Italian attack on Egypt was likely, insisted that all possible strength be gathered to resist it. One measure of his confidence in the defenses of Britain was his decision, while the Battle of Britain was at its height, to move the only remaining British armored units from England to Egypt.

In the first weeks of the war in North Africa, British raiding parties crossed the Cyrenaican frontier and achieved considerable success against Italian frontier posts. But in August an overwhelming force of Italians drove the British out of British Somaliland and threatened to move from Ethiopia into the Nile Valley. Churchill was much upset but could do nothing about it. In mid-September the Italians based in Cyrenaica advanced into Egypt as far as Sidi Barrani, then stopped to improve their supply situation and to build a pipeline for water.

British supplies for Egypt at this time traveled around the Cape of Good Hope and up through the Red Sea. Although the British had bases at both ends of the Mediterranean, at Gibraltar and at Alexandria, merchant ships could not hope to pass through the sea, even under convoy. The route passed close to Sicily and well within range of Italian aircraft, as well as through waters easily accessible to the Italian fleet. The British base at Malta, only 100 miles from Sicily, could provide little protection for British ships; its garrison was small, and even trying to get supplies through to the island was hazardous.

The British Admiralty was inclined to the view that all fleet elements should be withdrawn from the Eastern Mediterranean and concentrated at Gibraltar. But Churchill insisted that the fleet must stay at Alexandria and in fact should be strengthened with units that were better suited to operations there than to the defense of the home islands. The Chiefs of Staff Committee refused, however, to agree with his suggestion that an armored regiment en route to Egypt should travel from Gibraltar with a convoy of naval ships across the Mediterranean. At that time, as always, Churchill did not overrule his military chiefs when they were unanimous in opposing one of his imaginative ideas. Fortunately, the three-week delay of the long voyage around Africa did not jeopardize the situation in Egypt.

When the Free French, led by General Charles de Gaulle, wanted to consolidate a base in Africa from which to rally sup-

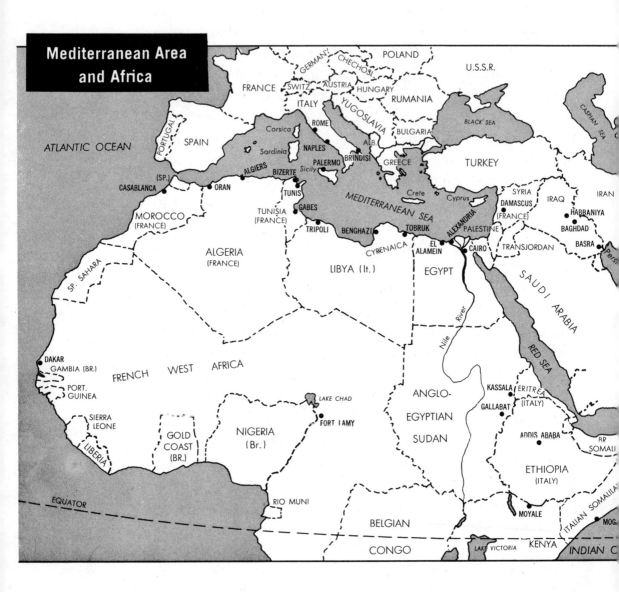

Mediterranean Area and Africa

ATLANTIC OCEAN

PORTUGAL
SPAIN
(SP.)
CASABLANCA
ORAN
ALGIERS
BIZERTE
TUNIS
Corsica
Sardinia
Sicily
NAPLES
PALERMO
BRINDISI
ROME
ITALY
FRANCE
SWITZ.
GERMANY
AUSTRIA HUNGARY
CHECHOSL.
POLAND
RUMANIA
YUGOSLAVIA
ALB.
BULGARIA
GREECE
BLACK SEA
U.S.S.R.
TURKEY
Crete
Cyprus
CASPIAN SEA

MOROCCO
(FRANCE)
TUNISIA
(FRANCE)
GABES
TRIPOLI
MEDITERRANEAN SEA
BENGHAZI
TOBRUK
ALEXANDRIA
CAIRO
EL ALAMEIN
PALESTINE
TRANSJORDAN
SYRIA
DAMASCUS
(FRANCE)
IRAQ
HABBANIYA
BAGHDAD
BASRA
IRAN
Pers.

ALGERIA
(FRANCE)
CYRENAICA
LIBYA (It.)
EGYPT
SAUDI ARABIA
RED SEA

SP. SAHARA
Nile River

DAKAR
GAMBIA (BR.)
PORT. GUINEA
FRENCH WEST AFRICA
LAKE CHAD
FORT LAMY
NIGERIA (Br.)
ANGLO-EGYPTIAN SUDAN
KASSALA
GALLABAT
ERITREA (ITALY)
ADDIS ABABA
BR. SOMALI

SIERRA LEONE
LIBERIA
GOLD COAST (BR.)
RIO MUNI
ETHIOPIA (ITALY)
MOYALE
ITALIAN SOMALILA
MOG.

EQUATOR
BELGIAN CONGO
LAKE VICTORIA
KENYA
INDIAN O.

118

port among the French colonies, Churchill enthusiastically endorsed their plan. He urged the War Cabinet to provide British troops and British naval vessels to support the Free French, despite the need for both to defend England. An attack on Dakar was planned for September 23. But word of the plan got to Vichy; naval and air reinforcements were sent to Dakar. The Allied attack was hampered by an unusual fog in the area, and frustrated by the unexpectedly strong resistance of the Vichy-French defenders. The operation was abandoned.

Italy attacked Greece on October 28, 1940, and the Greek government called on Britain for help. Churchill sent some air squadrons from Egypt, and British naval vessels moved into Suda Bay, the best harbor on the island of Crete, to prevent the Italians from taking it. No land forces could be spared for Greece, but they were not needed, for the Italians were soon repulsed by the valiant Greeks.

Victory in Cyrenaica

Churchill was eager to attack the Italians in the Western Desert between Egypt and Libya. To this end he urged General Sir Archibald Wavell, Middle East commander, to attack in Cyrenaica. He tried to send him all the forces that could be spared from England or elsewhere in the Middle East. Wavell attacked on December 6, and the Italians were soon surrendering by thousands or fleeing westward, pursued by the British. Bardia fell on January 5, 1941, and Tobruk two weeks later.

By mid-February Benghazi fell, and all of Cyrenaica was in British control. In the Sudan also, and in Eritrea, strengthened British forces pushed the Italians back.

Intelligence sources meanwhile had reported that the Germans were assembling troops in Rumania. From there they could easily march into Yugoslavia or through friendly Bulgaria to attack Greece. The Greeks had pushed the Italians back into Albania, but could not hope to withstand a determined German attack. Possession of Greece would give the Germans air bases in the Eastern Mediterranean and a stepping-stone toward Turkey and the Middle East.

Churchill placed support of Greece next in priority to securing the western flank of Egypt. Unfortunately the only forces available to send to Greece were those under General Wavell's command in North Africa. And until Benghazi was taken, none of these could be spared. Early in March, however, British troops began to move to Alexandria to be shipped to the assistance of Greece.

Tragedy in Greece

As it turned out, this British effort was also to be "too little and too late." On March 1 German troops moved into Bulgaria, and Bulgarian troops moved down to the Greek border. With attack imminent, the Greeks revised their strategic plans, including the use they would make of British troops coming from Egypt. Realistically they informed the British that the reinforcements would probably not suffice to stem a concerted German attack. This caused Churchill and the War Cabinet to consider dropping the operation, but they finally decided that Britain must honor its commitment to Greece to the extent possible. On March 5 the first units of the Expeditionary Force sailed from Alexandria for Greece.

Before swooping down on Greece, Hitler requested Yugoslavia to permit free passage for his armies. This was agreed on March 26, but the following day the Yugoslav government was deposed in a coup. The new government announced that it would resist any attempt by German troops to enter Yugoslavia. Hitler was so enraged by this act of defiance that he determined to destroy Yugoslavia. On April 6 German planes commenced a three-day raid on the capital, Belgrade, leaving it in smoking ruins with thousands of its citizens dead beneath the rubble. At the same time German soldiers swept across Yugoslavia's frontiers from Hungary, Rumania, and Bulgaria. The helpless Yugoslav government surrendered on April 17.

Nothing then stood in the way of a full-scale German assault on Greece, which had also been invaded on April 6. The Germans had command of the air as well as superiority on the ground, and the Greeks and British were no match for them. Pushed back down the peninsula, the Greek government capitulated on April 24. Despite constant, heavy air attacks, most of the British forces were evacuated from the southern Greek ports. Many of the evacuees were landed on Crete.

It was soon apparent that the Germans were anxious to take Crete and were accumulating a collection of small craft in

Greek harbors whose only purpose could be the carrying of invasion forces to the island. On May 20 German parachutists began dropping on the small island, in the sort of attack they had been hoping to make on England herself. Although the British fleet turned back or sank the vessels attempting to invade from the sea, the island's defenders were unable to repel the parachute troops, who landed in great numbers, although at great cost. Finally the hopeless defense was abandoned, and the fleet, under constant air attack, returned again and again to evacuate as many troops as possible.

Over five thousand Germans died in the Battle of Crete; the 7th Airborne Division was destroyed. Churchill, not knowing at the time that this was the only airborne division Hitler had, and impressed with its operation, ordered defenses prepared in Britain to cope with as many as four or five such divisions should Hitler try to use them against England.

Embattled Middle East

General Wavell had gravely depleted his own strength in order to send the expedition to Greece. He had further reduced the forces with which he held Cyrenaica by sending his 7th Armoured Division to Cairo for rest and to repair the tanks, since no replacements were at hand. Hitler, meanwhile, had sent some German troops under a most capable general, Erwin Rommel, to help his badly mauled allies in North Africa. On March 31 Rommel attacked the British outposts at Agheila and drove them back. It was soon evident to British leaders that this was not an Italian-type army but a German desert-trained force, led by a skillful general.

Although Churchill bombarded Wavell with telegrams, urging him to hold fast against the Germans, Wavell had no choice but to withdraw. Leaving a force in the rugged fortress of Tobruk, he pulled back into Egypt, making a stand near the border at Bardia and Salum. Rommel continued to attack, however, and took both these posts. Wavell moved back to a new line of defense east of Salum. The British defenders of Tobruk still held out, however, and were supplied and reinforced by sea.

Again Churchill thinned out the defenses of England to send reinforcements to the Middle East. He called on the navy to send more ships to the Mediterranean and to cut the Axis line of communications to North Africa. He urged that commandos be sent to attack the vital coastal road from Tripoli to Agheila and interrupt the German line of supply. But the military commanders were reluctant to risk disastrous losses which they feared would result from such operations. Wavell was also unwilling to risk his scanty forces in an attempt to relieve the garrison of Tobruk, despite Churchill's repeated urging.

As if there were not enough problems in the Eastern Mediterranean and the Middle East, at this time pro-German elements took over the government of Iraq. By treaty with Iraq, Britain was permitted to maintain important air bases at Basra on the Persian Gulf coast, and at Habbaniya near Baghdad. Fearing that these bases were threatened, Churchill called for reinforcements from India. On May 2, Iraqi forces attacked

Habbaniya. At once more men were transferred there by air from India. Despite Wavell's protests that he had insufficient forces, Churchill ordered him to send some ground units from his garrison in Palestine across the desert to Iraq. These forces attacked the Iraqis and drove them back to Baghdad, where the anti-British government capitulated on May 31.

The Vichy French meanwhile had been permitting Germans to cross through Syria into Iraq. To put a stop to this, and to help make the southern boundaries of Turkey secure from possible German pressure, Churchill ordered Wavell to seize Syria. Wavell somehow scraped together enough troops, including a Free French contingent, to invade Syria on June 8. The invasion was resisted by the Vichy garrison. By June 21, however, the Allied force had taken Damascus. The Vichy forces capitulated on July 12.

Despite the heavy losses Wavell's command had recently suffered in Greece and Crete, and in the far-flung operations of his forces in Iraq and Syria, Churchill continued to insist that his Middle East commander should launch a counteroffensive against Rommel in order to relieve the beleaguered garrison of Tobruk. After protesting that his exhausted forces were inadequate, Wavell loyally obeyed the Prime Minister's repeated demands. On June 15 he launched an attack on the Germans at Bardia and Salum, on the Egyptian-Cyrenaican border. But the assault was repulsed, and he was forced to withdraw into Egypt. Churchill reluctantly—and somewhat unfairly—decided that Wavell was exhausted by his efforts and discouraged by his defeats, and that a fresh commander was needed in the Middle

East. He sent Wavell to take command in India, and from India he brought General Sir Claude Auchinleck to replace Wavell.

Battle of the Atlantic

While dramatic action was taking place in the Middle East, the basic problem of providing food and military supplies to Britain remained always Churchill's main concern. He and Hitler both knew well that Britain was dependent upon her imports to survive as well as to make war. From the outset of hostilities German U-boats had been preying with increasing success on British shipping. German production was now turning out eighteen submarines every month and, as more of the raiders prowled the Atlantic sea-lanes, British shipping losses rose steadily.

Germany in 1940 controlled the European ports on the Atlantic Ocean from the northern tip of Norway to the Pyrenees in southern France. U-boats were not dependent, as they had been in World War I, on friendly ports overseas or on hazardous runs through the British blockade of the North Sea. They could refuel in French or Norwegian ports. They were also built to stay at sea much longer, and their torpedoes were much more deadly. Despite Churchill's efforts to develop measures to combat the U-boat menace, each month brought larger losses to England's vital shipping.

Early in March, 1941, Churchill decided to tackle the problem with even more concentrated effort. Terming the struggle the Battle of the Atlantic, he established a committee of high officials to study all aspects of the problem. Churchill called on the committee to develop ways of taking the offensive against U-boats at sea or in port, and also against the German Focke-Wulf bombers which were destroying merchant ships from the air. He called for fitting out merchant ships with fighter aircraft which could be launched to attack the bombers. He raised the question of whether planned modifications to the newly acquired American destroyers should be delayed until the critical period had passed. He asked for plans to assure concerted efforts to man merchant ships with the newest and best guns and crews, to defend the chief British ports, and to accelerate repairs on damaged vessels. And he requested that the committee study ways to reduce the time consumed in turnaround of shipping in Britain, to increase the supply of laborers on docks and in shipyards, and to eliminate congestion on the wharves of London.

Since the beginning of the war, merchant ships had been traveling in convoys. But the use of escorts was limited by the number of destroyers available and by their range without refueling. A number of developments eased these problems in early 1941. The intensive Canadian shipbuilding program began to produce more escort vessels, and the Canadian navy could take a more active part in escorting. New bases in Newfoundland, Greenland, and Iceland placed supplies of fuel for destroyers and other escorts at strategic points.

President Roosevelt, aware that Britain was fighting in defense of the entire free world, but realizing that his nation was not yet ready to enter the war, stretched the United States' status as a nonbelligerent in various ways. The concept of lend-lease opened a vast source of supplies for which the British would not have to pay until after the war, thus enabling Churchill to conserve Britain's dwindling resources. American bases in British possessions brought the United States Navy closer to the Atlantic shipping lanes.

Roosevelt established a line of demarcation between Eastern and Western Hemispheres in the middle of the Atlantic Ocean. American warships thereafter patrolled west of that line in defense of the Western Hemisphere, searching for U-boats and German surface raiders, reducing the vast area which the British had to patrol. Finally the establishment of a United States naval base in Iceland enabled United States warships to escort convoys that far from American ports.

Alliance with Russia

At the end of March intelligence reports reaching London showed increasing evidence that Hitler was getting ready to attack Russia. As pieces of intelligence were matched together the imminence of the attack became clearer, and in April Churchill sent a warning to Stalin, who apparently did not believe it. Two months later, on June 22, the German armies invaded Russia.

Despite Churchill's long and consistent opposition to communism, to Stalin, and to the Soviet Union, he did not for a moment doubt that Britain must now join hands with the Russians in the common fight against the archenemy, Adolf Hitler. In a speech to the British people he reiterated the determination to carry on.

We have but one aim and one single, irrevocable purpose. We are resolved to destroy Hitler and every vestige of the Nazi regime. From this nothing will turn us— nothing. We will never parley, we will never negotiate with Hitler or any of his gang. We shall fight him by land, we shall fight him by sea, we shall fight him in the air, until, with God's help, we have rid the earth of his shadow and liberated its people from his yoke. Any man or state who fights on against Nazidom will have our aid. Any man or state who marches with Hitler is our foe. . . . It follows, therefore, that we shall give whatever help we can to Russia and the Russian people.

CHAPTER 9

The Grand Alliance

Aid to Russia

Although the German attack on Russia consumed most of the German war effort, reducing pressure on Britain, the new alliance with the Soviet Union was not an unmixed blessing. Churchill soon found that Joseph Stalin was a very difficult man to deal with and that he had definite views on what the British could and should do to help the Russians.

Supplies of badly needed munitions were just beginning to flow from the United States to Britain. At last it had become possible to plan on sending tanks and planes and men to the Middle East to build up a force strong enough to challenge the Germans in the Western Desert. But with Germans pouring into Russia, and with the poorly equipped Russian armies being overwhelmed, much of the new and modern equipment and the materials for war industry had to be diverted to the Soviet Union. Stalin demanded it, and since his armies were fighting and killing Germans, it would have been difficult to refuse what could possibly be spared.

Churchill therefore sacrificed much of the material and

equipment he had long awaited, shipping the fruits of British and American production on to Russia by way of Murmansk and Archangel. But he could not help being irritated when Stalin at once demanded that the British open a second front in Europe immediately. Churchill patiently explained in messages to the Soviet dictator that a landing large enough to help the Russians could not possibly succeed before much planning had been completed and great supplies of men and equipment had been assembled. But Stalin could not or would not accept the explanation, and kept repeating his calls for a British invasion of the Continent.

This attitude was typical of Stalin's ideas on military cooperation. Although demanding information on British plans and intentions, Stalin refused to tell his allies anything of Russian plans or military strengths or dispositions. Stalin's demands for military assistance were based entirely on wishful thinking, with no regard for the practical problems involved in opening a second front in the Balkans, or of shipping twenty-five to thirty British divisions to Russia through Archangel or Iran, both schemes which Stalin suggested in the summer of 1941. Churchill's attempts to arrange for cooperation between the top-level military staffs accomplished nothing.

Only one joint British-Soviet military action was taken: the occupation of Iran by British and Russian troops. This operation resulted in expulsion of the Germans who were influencing the Iranian government, and it secured the valuable Iranian oil fields for the Allies. Above all, it developed a supply route to

Russia from the port of Basra to the Caucasus and the Caspian Sea.

President and Prime Minister

In the first week of August, 1941, Churchill sailed across the Atlantic aboard the newest British battleship, *Prince of Wales*, for Placentia Bay, in Newfoundland. There he met with President Roosevelt aboard the United States cruiser *Augusta*. They were accompanied by the military chiefs of both nations who also conferred separately. This, the first of many similar meetings, resulted in a statement of the ultimate objectives of the nation that was at war and the nation that was furnishing non-belligerent support. Churchill wrote the first draft of this document, known as The Atlantic Charter, and both he and Roosevelt and their staffs contributed to the revisions.

Churchill found President Roosevelt preoccupied with the situation in the Far East, where Japan seemed to be threatening to extend her already sizable expansion at the expense of the other nations in the area. On July 26 the United States had imposed economic sanctions against Japan, to reduce her potential for aggression in Asia, and to warn Japanese leaders of American determination. Churchill had promptly taken the same step, for British colonies were among the possible Japanese objectives.

Japan's reaction had been to ask for negotiations and suggest terms she would accept. Although the terms were unacceptable to the United States, Roosevelt and Churchill agreed that negotiations would gain time for the Americans to strengthen their defenses of the Philippines and for the British to improve their position in Singapore, probable targets of Japanese attack. Churchill drafted a warning, which Roosevelt agreed to use, that "any further encroachment by Japan in the Southwest Pacific would produce a situation in which the United States Government would be compelled to take counter-measures, even though these might lead to war between the United States and Japan." Should this come, Churchill assured Roosevelt, Britain would also at once declare war on Japan.

Renewed Activity in the Western Desert

It was a source of some embarrassment to Churchill, particularly in his dealings with Stalin, that during the summer of 1941 British forces in Egypt were inactive. He had urged General Auchinleck as soon as he took command to plan for an offensive at the earliest possible time. He repeatedly pointed out to Auchinleck that while the Germans were busy in Russia they could not send sizable reinforcements to General Rommel. Both for practical military reasons and for the psychological effect it seemed like a good time to attack.

Auchinleck welcomed the reinforcements that were beginning to arrive but insisted that he would not be ready to attack until his combat and reserve strength was increased, and his men were well trained in the use of the new American tanks. Reluctantly, Churchill and the War Cabinet accepted Auchinleck's plan for an offensive on November 1.

Auchinleck's position was improved by British naval action in the Mediterranean. German air forces based in Crete and in Libya had made the route from Alexandria to Malta so hazardous that supplies for that island had to be sent through from Gibraltar, the route that had earlier been considered too dangerous. But now the German air force had been called from Sicily to Russia. The base on Malta was strengthened, and a naval raiding force was stationed there at Churchill's insistence. These ships, supported by planes operating from the carrier *Ark Royal* and from Maltese bases, had considerable success in attacking Rommel's supply ships passing from Sicily to North Africa. In August, 33 percent of the supplies being sent to Rommel were lost; by October this figure reached 63 percent. This success shortly came to an end, however, for the Germans sent U-boats into the Mediterranean in November, and German air power was returned to Sicily. The first important U-boat victim was the *Ark Royal*.

Churchill's eagerness for action, and victory, in the Western Desert was part of a larger scheme he developed in the late summer of 1941. Should Rommel be defeated and driven back through Libya, then the French garrisons in Tunisia, Algeria, and Morocco might well desert Vichy and join the Allies. Perhaps even Vichy might join. If none of this developed, the possession of Tripolitania would at least provide a base from which to step via Malta to Sicily and Italy, and there open a second front in Europe.

Ambitious though this strategic project might seem, Italy was the only area on the Continent, except possibly Norway, where the British could hope to assault the Continent without drawing German forces toward the vital lifeline across the Atlantic or toward England herself. The British Chiefs of Staff and their Planning Committee carefully worked out plans to invade Sicily, should opportunity offer.

British commanders in the Middle East took a dim view of Churchill's idea of an invasion of Sicily. Because of their objections, it was agreed that if Auchinleck defeated Rommel in Cyrenaica, he should move on to Tripoli. From there, if the French invited it, he could continue into French Northwest Africa. Two infantry divisions and an armored division would stand ready to support whatever action developed.

Auchinleck's forces attacked on November 18, five days before Rommel had planned to make a new assault on Tobruk. Although he was surprised, Rommel fought back hard. The battle displayed his great ability as a general and won the admiration of his British opponents as he repulsed the British attacks and then counterattacked. However, his lack of the equipment and supplies that had been sent to the bottom of the Mediterranean soon exhausted his scanty reserves, and the British pushed him back to the border of Tripolitania.

On December 31 Rommel dug in at Agheila. Auchinleck's forces were exhausted by their pursuit across the Western Desert and were short of supplies because of their distance from their Egyptian bases. They were also depleted by the necessity to leave sizable forces behind to contend with the German garrisons bypassed at Bardia and Salum. Auchinleck therefore paused to wait for the capture of these posts, and to build up supplies before renewing the attack.

Outbreak of the Pacific War

Meanwhile, on December 7 and 8, the Japanese attacks on Pearl Harbor and Malaya changed the whole strategic picture.

Fully occupied as the British were with the war against Germany, little could be spared for defense of British colonies in the Far East. However, in accordance with his agreement with Roosevelt, Churchill had already sent some land and air reinforcements to Malaya and Burma. But he believed that a show of naval force might prove the best deterrent to Japanese aggression. Over Admiralty protest he had insisted that the newly built battleship *Prince of Wales* and the battle cruiser *Repulse*, rather than slower and less modern ships, be sent to the Indian Ocean. They would be followed by others, to provide naval protection to British colonies and supply routes in the East.

As soon as Churchill heard of the attack on Pearl Harbor, he telephoned Roosevelt to promise that Britain would at once declare war on Japan. The nearly simultaneous Japanese attacks on Malaya, Singapore, and Hong Kong gave him more than adequate reason to fulfill the promise. With Hitler's declaration of war on the United States on December 11, at last Britain had the strong ally Churchill had hoped for. He had already prepared the atmosphere and the procedure for close cooperation. At once he proposed to Roosevelt that he go to Washington to discuss joint strategic plans for the war and for the numerous problems of production and distribution of war materials.

One important reason for the trip was to make certain that the United States would not waver from the informal understandings reached during the Atlantic Conference. At that time Churchill, Roosevelt, and their military advisers had agreed that in the event America entered the war against Germany, and was simultaneously engaged in war with Japan, the first priority of the Allies must be the defeat of the more dangerous enemy: Germany. Churchill feared that American reaction to the treacherous attack on Pearl Harbor might cause the United States government to concentrate its efforts against Japan.

Before Churchill left London he received word that the base of his strategic thinking about the Far East had been destroyed. The *Prince of Wales* and the *Repulse* were both sunk by Japanese air attack on December 10. Despite this blow, however, his views remained unchanged—Hitler was the prime enemy.

The "Arcadia" Conference

As Churchill traveled westward across the Atlantic in the battleship *Duke of York*, he wrote down his thoughts on future strategy. The war could be ended, he thought, only by defeating German armies in Europe or through a revolt of the German people. As soon as the Allies were strong enough they must land in Western and Southern Europe. Their appearance in the occupied countries, he believed, would cause the local populations to rise and help overthrow their German conquerors. But this could not come before 1943, at the earliest. In the meantime, control of North Africa lay within Allied grasp, and with it control of the Mediterranean.

Churchill was hopeful that pressure on the Vichy government and the French authorities in northern Africa would deliver French North Africa to the Allied cause and result in the transfer of the French fleet from Toulon to North African ports. Should the French refuse to cooperate, North Africa should be taken by force in 1942. Plans should be prepared at once to seize the Atlantic ports of Morocco and French West Africa.

In the Pacific in 1942, Churchill foresaw nothing but further disaster as long as Japan enjoyed naval superiority. But he believed that every bit of territory should be defended to the utmost and that every attempt should be made to support the defenders. He thought that by May, 1942, a superior battle fleet could be formed in the Pacific, built around battleships and as many aircraft carriers as possible. (He was not yet aware of the magnitude of American losses at Pearl Harbor.) If there were not enough large carriers, he somewhat unrealistically believed that others could be improvised, even if they could carry no more than a dozen planes. Some action in the Pacific could be undertaken in 1942, but not at the expense of the North African program, or the buildup against Germany. The defeat

Churchill and President Roosevelt chatting at the "Arcadia" Conference in Washington, D.C. (Franklin D. Roosevelt Library, Hyde Park, New York)

of Germany would bring about the defeat of Japan, he believed. But an earlier defeat of Japan would have little effect on the war against Germany.

When the conference—known as "Arcadia"—opened in Washington, Churchill was relieved to discover that the Americans, for all their eagerness to strike back at Japan, still agreed that Germany was the prime enemy. An operation in North Africa was accepted in principle; planning, under the code name "Gymnast," was to proceed. Two United States divisions were to be sent to Northern Ireland to release more experienced British divisions for "Gymnast," and United States bombers were to start operating from bases in Britain as soon as possible. In the Pacific it was agreed that an attempt should be made to regain the initiative. This would be a United States responsibility. Now aware of American weaknesses in the Pacific, Churchill visualized the action there as a series of commando-type raids.

Perhaps the greatest accomplishment at "Arcadia" was the establishment of machinery to coordinate the planning of the two military staffs, through a committee known as the Combined Chiefs of Staff. Throughout the war permanent representatives of the British Chiefs of Staff remained in Washington, where they met on a regular basis with the newly established U.S. Joint Chiefs of Staff. From that time on, the Combined Chiefs of Staff directed the overall strategy of the war, subject when necessary to approval by the President and the Prime Minister.

During Churchill's Washington visit he was invited to address a joint session of the United States Congress, an honor which he greatly prized. Early in his talk he confirmed his place in the hearts of Americans by saying:

> The fact that my American forebears have for so many generations played their part in the life of the United States, and that here I am, an Englishman, welcomed in your midst, makes this experience one of the most moving and thrilling in my life, which is already long and has not been entirely uneventful. I wish indeed that my mother,

139

whose memory I cherish across the vale of years, could have been here to see. By the way, I cannot help reflecting that if my father had been American and my mother British, instead of the other way around, I might have got here on my own.

Japanese Victories

As Churchill had expected, the Japanese attacks spread against British, Dutch, and American possessions in Southeast Asia and the East Indies. At "Arcadia" General Wavell was put in command of the combined American, British, Dutch, and Australian forces in the area, although there was little hope that his ABDA Command—as it was called—could resist the onrushing Japanese.

Churchill kept close track of the fighting in Malaya. One division from England was en route to Singapore, but as the Japanese advanced inexorably down the peninsula, he tried in vain to find more reinforcements to send to Wavell. When the Prime Minister learned to his horrified surprise that the fortress at Singapore, which he had believed impregnable, had most of its guns so placed that they could fire only toward the sea, he sent the local commanders numerous suggestions for improvising defenses against the attack that was approaching on the landward side.

As the outnumbered defenders withdrew down the peninsula toward Singapore, Churchill repeatedly urged in the old British tradition, "The battle must be fought to the bitter end at all costs. . . . Commanders and senior officers should die with their troops. The honour of the British Empire and of the British Army is at stake." But when supplies of food and water in the city ran low, and it was apparent that the fortress could not hold out, he gave permission to surrender. About 85,000 men became prisoners of the Japanese.

Although defense was stubborn, the Japanese land and sea forces could not be held back from Burma and the islands of the Dutch East Indies. Churchill was determined, however, to hold India and Ceylon and the vital approaches to the Middle East. He rushed reinforcements to the area to prevent any possibility of a link-up of German and Japanese forces in the Middle East.

Anglo-American Strategic Debates

Meanwhile, the American Joint Chiefs of Staff decided that they did not like Churchill's proposed North African operation. They wanted to attempt an earlier landing in Europe instead. They believed that the Allied potential could best be realized in Western Europe, where they could more directly threaten Germany, the main foe. Furthermore, an assault in Northwest Europe would afford maximum support to Russia. They thought that an attack on France with forty-eight divisions could be made in April, 1943, or if shipping problems delayed it, at least by late summer. All major Allied efforts in 1942 should go into preparation for that attack. In April, 1942, President Roosevelt sent General George C. Marshall, Army Chief of Staff, and his personal representative, Mr. Harry Hopkins, to London to present the American views.

Churchill agreed with the idea of planning for a full-scale invasion of the Continent in 1943, but with certain reservations. India must be defended and Japan prevented from linking up with Germany through India or the Middle East. He disliked the idea of the combined forces of England and the United States sitting idle for a year and a half while the buildup for landings on the Continent proceeded. Again he promoted the idea of "Gymnast," the North African operation. Alternatively, or in addition, he favored an attack on northern Norway, which he thought could be done cheaply and would open a supply route to Russia to replace the highly hazardous sea route to Murmansk.

To General Marshall these operations seemed diversionary. He proposed an attack on Brest or Cherbourg ("Sledgehammer" was the code name for the operation) for the fall of 1942. Although Churchill thought this scheme impractical, he agreed to let planning proceed for "Sledgehammer."

The British planners soon found that there were great hazards involved in "Sledgehammer" and raised the question of whether such an operation would be worth the cost. Churchill thought it would not. Since no one but he had much interest in the Norway operation, he preferred to concentrate on a large cross-Channel invasion in 1943 ("Roundup"). In fact, he thought there should be at least six large-scale landings and the same number of feints, at various points in Denmark, Holland, Belgium, the Pas-de-Calais, the Cotentin Peninsula, and at Brest, St.-Nazaire, and the mouth of the Gironde River.

So unworkable did "Sledgehammer" seem to the British that in June Churchill flew to the United States to confer with Roosevelt on plans for 1942–43. He could not get a final decision satisfactory to both sides. However they agreed to proceed with the buildup for "Roundup" on as large a scale as possible, and to continue planning for "Sledgehammer" and studying the feasibility of "Gymnast," and operations in Norway or in the Iberian Peninsula if "Sledgehammer" should prove unworkable.

Churchill's visit to Washington coincided with Rommel's capture of Tobruk, climaxing a German offensive that had been launched on January 21 and had steadily driven the British back toward Egypt. Churchill had been watching the operations in the Mediterranean and North Africa closely, urging Auchinleck to attack, and calling for every effort to supply and strengthen the garrison on the strategic island of Malta. He had ordered all the reinforcements he could find to Egypt. When word of the fall of Tobruk reached him, he asked his American hosts for help and was delighted when General Marshall offered three hundred new Sherman tanks.

Back in London in July, Churchill was more than ever convinced that "Sledgehammer" was impracticable. The occupation of northwest Africa seemed even more attractive. There, he felt, American and British soldiers could fight Germans in 1942 and gain control of the strategic Mediterranean area, while awaiting the accumulation of men and equipment for

"Roundup" the following year. "Gymnast" could be done, and there would still be forces enough to land in Norway.

In Washington, although Roosevelt was inclined to like the idea of an operation in North Africa, both General Marshall and Admiral Ernest J. King, Chief of Naval Operations, disagreed. They had four major objections: (1) "Gymnast" would require the diversion of naval forces, particularly aircraft carriers, from the Pacific; (2) it would require a new line of communications across the Atlantic with all the problems of a new convoy system; (3) landings on the Atlantic coast at Casablanca alone would not help Russia and landings inside the Mediterranean would be too hazardous; (4) the commitment to "Gymnast" would destroy any possibility of undertaking "Roundup" in 1943. "Sledgehammer," they thought, would be a much better project for 1942.

Roosevelt decided to send Marshall and King to London to debate the issue. He refused to accept their recommendation that if the British would not agree on "Sledgehammer" the main American effort should be transferred to the Pacific. He insisted that they must reach agreement with the British on some operation for 1942. So it was, after long argument, that Churchill's North Africa operation, which he promptly renamed "Torch," was adopted.

Shortly after this, Churchill flew to Moscow for his first meeting with Stalin. He found the Russian premier unhappy at the abandonment of "Sledgehammer," but Churchill finally convinced him of the advantages of "Torch."

Operation "Torch"

Upon Churchill's return to London he immersed himself in planning for "Torch." American General Dwight D. Eisenhower had been chosen commander in chief of the operation, and at Churchill's request Eisenhower kept him fully informed of the progress of preparations. Churchill viewed the occupation of North Africa as the first step of a larger plan to attack Italy and knock her out of the war. His concept involved the occupation of Algeria and Tunisia, the latter possibly by an attack from the east after Libya was in British hands. Churchill thought the British should attack Algiers; the Americans should take Oran and, if they thought it wise, Casablanca, on the Atlantic shore.

In late August, Churchill discovered that while Eisenhower's staff had been proceeding in accordance with the program as he saw it, the U.S. Joint Chiefs in Washington were planning only to attack Casablanca and Oran. They disliked the hazards of depending on a narrow supply route through the Strait of Gibraltar and preferred to make the major landing on the open Atlantic coast.

Roosevelt surprised Churchill by telling him he thought the initial attacks should be made entirely by American forces, for he thought the French would be less likely to resist if the attackers were not British. About a week after the landings at Oran and Casablanca, he suggested, the British could make their landings in Algiers. Churchill was well aware that the Vichy government was not very fond of Britain, but he was not convinced that it was fond enough of the United States to mean the difference between resistance and submission. Moreover, the planners in England were finding it necessary to use large numbers of British troops and planes, and to call on Britain to supply most of the transportation and two-thirds of the naval force. Churchill believed that if anything was to be given up, it should be Casablanca, for the hazards of landing on an open shore would not be offset by the results of a successful attack in that area, far from the Mediterranean.

The delays in preparations caused by this disagreement made Churchill impatient, and he urged that a decision be reached promptly and a date be set for the operation. Since it was apparent that Roosevelt would not give up on Casablanca, Churchill recommended cutting down the plan in order to provide enough men and shipping for all three objectives. A compromise was finally reached and preparations for a three-pronged attack proceeded.

In the early dawn of November 8, 1942, the landing craft headed for the beaches. At Casablanca the invaders met stiff resistance; less opposition was encountered at Algiers and Oran. The last defenders in all three areas surrendered on November 11, and the French colonies were in Allied hands. A week before, Rommel had been defeated in the great battle of El Alamein, and forced once more to withdraw to the west. Control of all of North Africa was within the grasp of the Allies.

Although much hard fighting lay ahead before Tunisia would be taken and the Germans captured or driven from the south shore of the Mediterranean, Churchill was eager to move on from the base the Allies would soon have. He did not think that "Torch" had made "Sledgehammer" impossible for 1943, and he favored at least feints on the northern shores of France. But from Tunisia it was only a step across the Mediterranean to Sicily and Sardinia, and from those bases inviting targets beckoned in Italy and southern France. In such a program the Allies could draw Germans away from the Russian front, knock Italy out of the war, and avoid the risks of a costly operation on the well-defended shores of France before an overwhelming Allied force was ready to undertake the final assault.

The Strategic Debate Continues

Churchill's thinking was not shared by the Americans. They saw little to be gained by involvement in the Mediterranean when it was agreed that France would be the main battle-ground. Because of the diversion to North Africa, a large-scale attack across the English Channel in 1943 seemed to them to be impossible. Therefore it should be postponed until 1944 and nothing should be allowed to interfere with it.

It was obvious that these basic strategic issues must be settled, and Roosevelt and Churchill met at Casablanca in January, 1943, to talk them over. Most of Churchill's views were adopted. The buildup of forces in England was to be continued, in order that advantage might be taken of any early

The Prime Minister talking with President Roosevelt on the lawn of the President's villa at Casablanca. (U. S. Army)

opportunity to reenter the Continent through France. The heaviest possible air offensive was to be carried out against targets in Germany and occupied Europe. The North African base would be used for an assault on Sicily, in order to divert German pressure from Russia, to increase Allied pressure on Italy, and to secure the line of communications through the Mediterranean. Without jeopardizing the buildup in Britain, or the Sicilian operation, pressure was also to be maintained on Japan and preparations made to recapture Burma later in the year.

The late winter and spring of 1943 saw victories in Russia, where the Germans were repulsed at Stalingrad and pushed back all along the line. In Africa, the British attackers from the east, now commanded by General Sir Harold Alexander, joined American and British forces moving in from the west. Together they pinned the dwindling German and Italian forces into the bulge of Tunisia. On May 13, the last Axis elements in North Africa surrendered.

In anticipation of this victory, Churchill and his staff had sailed on the *Queen Mary* for the United States on May 4, to discuss with Roosevelt how the victory should be exploited, and what should be done in Burma.

There was no doubt in Churchill's mind as to what should follow the capture of Sicily—an assault on Italy. Knocking Italy out of the war would probably not cause the immediate collapse of Germany, but it might be the beginning of the end. Moreover it would have other desirable results in the Mediterranean. Churchill had tried in vain to persuade Turkey to support the Allied cause; now she might decide to permit the use of bases in her territory. In the Balkans there were some twenty-five Italian divisions whose withdrawal on the collapse of Italy would force Hitler either to send German divisions there from the Russian front or give up the area. Elimination of Italy and the Italian fleet would release British battleships and aircraft carriers for operations in the Bay of Bengal or the Pacific. Nowhere else, said Churchill, could the Allies do so much in 1943, and give so much help to the Russians, as they could in Italy.

Churchill was not opposed to the idea of a cross-Channel operation, although, like many American planners, he now thought it would have to be postponed until 1944. Undoubtedly remembering the failure at Gallipoli, where preparations had been inadequate, he wanted to be sure before a full-scale invasion of Europe was launched that it was based on the most meticulous and thorough planning to assure the most favorable prospect of success.

In Washington, Churchill found that the President did not share his conviction of the desirability of attacking Italy. Roosevelt, like his military chiefs, thought that after Sicily was taken. all excess troops should be put into the buildup in Britain, in preparation for the invasion of the Continent in the spring of 1944. Although Churchill stayed in Washington for two weeks, and the combined staffs met many times, they made no definite decision on what operation should follow Sicily. They agreed only to plan to exploit that occupation in the manner that would be most likely to eliminate Italy from the war and to keep Germans occupied.

Churchill was well aware that Marshall had never liked the idea of going into North Africa and was now opposed to attacking Italy. He determined to win Marshall over. Since Churchill was planning to go from Washington to North Africa to confer with the local military commanders, he invited Marshall to accompany him. Somewhat surprised, the austere American general accepted.

At Algiers the two men met with Eisenhower, as well as with General Alexander and other British leaders. The British had by far the largest military force in the area, and they were eager to push on to continue the fight. The British commanders shared Churchill's desire not to let these armies sit idle for a year until all was in readiness to cross the Channel. They accepted Churchill's view that Italy should be the next objective.

General Eisenhower was also in favor of continuing action after seizing Sicily, but he was inclined to think that Sardinia or Corsica would be preferable to Italy as the next target. If victory came easily in Sicily, however, he would be willing to go from there to Italy, and he agreed that it would be desirable to eliminate Italy from the war. General Marshall, however, remained unwilling to commit himself to a campaign in Italy, and Churchill accepted a decision to wait until the Sicilian operation was under way before selecting the next objective.

Sicily and "Quadrant"

Allied forces landed in Sicily on July 10, 1943. Their progress was so rapid and resistance so weak that Eisenhower decided that they should move on into Italy. The Combined Chiefs of Staff authorized planning for an assault on the Naples area ("Avalanche"), as well as several smaller landings around the heel and toe of the peninsula. On July 25, Mussolini was unexpectedly dismissed as Premier by the King of Italy. The Combined Chiefs then directed Eisenhower to launch "Avalanche" as soon as possible, coordinated with an attack on Italy's toe. Despite their agreement to this operation, the American chiefs remained insistent on the priority of the buildup in

The Allied Conference at Quebec, August 1943. Seated are Canadian Prime Minister Mackenzie King, President Roosevelt, and Churchill. Top military and naval chiefs stand behind the three principals as United States, Canadian, and British flags fly over the historic Citadel in background. (U. S. Army)

152

Britain. They insisted that Eisenhower should operate with what he had, with a minimum of additional support.

With Italy firm as the next objective, Churchill thought it was time for another meeting with Roosevelt. In August the two staffs assembled at Quebec, for the conference known as "Quadrant." By then a great deal of planing for the cross-Channel attack had been completed, and it was generally agreed that the target date for a landing in Normandy should be May, 1944.

Until "Quadrant" it had been expected that the commander in chief for the invasion of France—now called "Overlord"—should be British, since the commander of "Torch" was American. But it was now evident that although the numbers in the original landings would be about equally divided between British and Americans, the follow-up forces would be predominantly American. Consequently, Churchill suggested, and Roosevelt agreed, that the command should be given to an American, although no individual was yet suggested. This decision was a bitter disappointment to General Sir Alan Brooke, Chief of the Imperial General Staff, who had expected the appointment, and who felt that Churchill had promised it to him. As his memoirs reveal, Brooke—later Lord Alanbrooke—never forgave Churchill, although he continued to perform loyally and well his duties in the War Office and on the Chiefs of Staff Committee.

Much of the discussion at "Quadrant" centered around the war against Japan. Earlier decisions to undertake major land operations in north Burma, in order to open an overland route into China, had not been attractive to Churchill, who did not like the idea of large British forces becoming involved in protracted jungle fighting. He preferred to wait until enough landing craft were available for an amphibious attack across the Bay of Bengal on the Malay Peninsula or, even better, against Sumatra, which would afford bases for attacks on Japanese shipping and Japanese bases in Southeast Asia.

The Americans were in favor of seizing Burma and thus acquiring easier access to Chinese bases for air and amphibious operations against Japan. Churchill proposed that an attempt be made to coordinate action in the area and accomplish something worthwhile by setting up a coordinated Allied command. His proposal was accepted and the Southeast Asia Command was created at "Quadrant," with Admiral Lord Louis Mountbatten as Supreme Allied Commander. Wavell was to remain Commander in Chief, India.

Surrender of Italy

Mussolini's departure from the Italian government had been followed by negotiations between the new Prime Minister, Marshal Pietro Badoglio, and the Allies, which lasted for weeks. On Churchill's urging, Roosevelt and Stalin agreed that the Italians should be given the status of cobelligerents and asked to fight against their former German allies.

On September 8, Badoglio announced the Italian surrender. At the same time the Italian fleet sailed to Malta—attacked by

German planes on the way—and surrendered, thereby eliminating a naval threat and adding to the Allied fleets.

The Germans, unwilling to give up Italy, had kidnapped Mussolini, who was being held prisoner in northern Italy, and set him up as leader of a rival government. This resulted in a civil war. Hitler at once sent more troops to occupy Italy in strength. Meanwhile, the German commander in Italy, Field Marshal Albert Kesselring, deployed his available forces to meet the expected Allied amphibious assault near Naples. When Allied troops landed on the beaches at Salerno on September 9, they found themselves confronting strong German divisions and faced with a long, hard fight up the peninsula.

Churchill Looks to the Eastern Mediterranean

Churchill had long believed in the importance of gaining control of the Eastern Mediterranean and of persuading Turkey to join the Allied cause. His most important objectives in that area were to gain air bases and to get access through the Dardanelles to the Black Sea and Russia. The opportunity seemed at hand to seize strategic islands in the Aegean that were wholly or partly held by Italian garrisons before the Germans could reinforce or replace them. Rhodes, Leros, and Cos in particular had air bases as well as ports that would provide protection for the Mediterranean Fleet. Control of the Aegean, he thought, would tip Turkey into the Allied camp.

Stimulated by Churchill, plans for an assault on Rhodes had

been drawn up by the Middle East Command early in 1943, and a division in Egypt was preparing to attack the island on September 1. But a few days before that the Combined Chiefs of Staff ordered the necessary shipping for the landings to be sent to India as planned for operations against Burma. The division in Egypt was ordered to join the Allied forces in the Central Mediterranean.

Churchill hesitated to interfere with the shipping diversion, to which he had agreed at Washington in May, but he urged the Middle East Commander, General Sir Henry Maitland Wilson, to try to do something with what remaining forces he had. Accordingly, Wilson sent a small airborne mission to Rhodes to try to secure the island's surrender. But the Italian garrison there stuck with the Germans, and the British force had to be evacuated from the island. When other small forces were put ashore on Samos and Cos, the Germans landed troops by air and quickly overwhelmed the British expeditions.

Despite these failures, the importance of Rhodes and the Aegean increased in Churchill's mind. He saw it as a key area, controlling not only the approaches to the Dardanelles, but the Balkans as well. Germany had a large number of divisions in the Balkans, and Churchill thought that if the Allies could gain a foothold as close as the Aegean, Hitler would be forced to send more troops to the area in order to prevent the local populations from revolting. Allied air forces in the Aegean islands would also draw German air strength to the Balkans and offer a new opportunity to shoot down German planes.

In order to take Rhodes and hold it, Churchill needed men

and landing craft, and he strongly urged Roosevelt to agree that they be provided. But Roosevelt was not convinced by Churchill's arguments. He interpreted the Rhodes operation as the first step in a new strategic picture that would be followed by occupation of Cos and Crete, since both were within air range of Rhodes, and probably would lead to an invasion of the Balkans. Roosevelt and his military advisers thought it was more important to concentrate on taking Italy, and then doing "Overlord," than to become involved in the Eastern Mediterranean and the Balkans. Although Churchill insisted that the diversion of men and shipping would be temporary, Roosevelt refused to agree that they could be diverted from either of the other operations.

"Sextant" and "Eureka"

In November, 1943, Roosevelt and Churchill and their staffs met again, this time at Cairo, for a conference code-named "Sextant." At Cairo they were joined, at Roosevelt's insistence, by Generalissimo Chiang Kai-shek. From Cairo Roosevelt and Churchill went on to Teheran, where Marshal Stalin met with them for three days in the "Eureka" Conference. They then returned to Cairo to complete the "Sextant" discussions.

Churchill was disappointed in the results of the Cairo meetings where the presence of the Chinese led to long talks about that theater, which he considered secondary. He was stunned when the President promised Chiang an Anglo-American amphibious operation across the Bay of Bengal to coincide with land operations in Burma. Although Churchill was anxious to reoccupy the Malay Peninsula or Sumatra, he realized that such an operation in 1944 would require landing craft that were earmarked for "Overlord" or that could be used to better advantage, in his view, against the Italian coast or elsewhere in the Mediterranean. Eventually Roosevelt was convinced of this and the promise was retracted, much to the annoyance of Chiang Kai-shek.

The Allies were still unable to agree on the future course of action in the Mediterranean. It had earlier been decided that operations in Italy should halt at the Pisa-Rimini line, after capturing Rome and the air bases from which strategic bombers could strike vital German targets. The advance was going more slowly than had been hoped, but even so it was expected that the line would be reached some months before "Overlord" was launched. Then, by going on the defensive, Allied force requirements in Italy would be greatly reduced.

There was no shipping available to move the surplus troops from Italy in time for the "Overlord" buildup. Part of them, Churchill thought, could best be used for gaining control of the Aegean and the Eastern Mediterranean. The Americans, however, thought that such troops should be landed in southern France, in an operation to be coordinated with "Overlord," which would be followed by an advance up the Rhone Valley to join the forces landed in Normandy.

Roosevelt had suggested that troops might be landed at the head of the Adriatic to open an advance toward the Danube

Marshal Stalin, President Roosevelt, and Prime Minister Churchill at the Teheran Conference. (UPI)

and Vienna. This appealed to Churchill more than the proposed landings in southern France. But neither of these operations would come for six months or more. In the meantime, Churchill urged, the Eastern Mediterranean could be made secure, using some of the troops from Italy. Some help could also be sent to Yugoslav and Greek guerrilla fighters in the Balkans, who, with little support, were pinning down a large number of Germans. Preparation for "Overlord" called for removing most of the landing craft from the Mediterranean, but Churchill thought that if enough were kept for an additional six weeks or so to move two divisions, they could be put to better use than sitting in Britain.

Churchill repeatedly raised the question of getting Turkey into the war, of retaining landing craft in the Mediterranean, and of using the troops in the area during the interval before "Overlord" could be launched to gain control of the Aegean and to help the guerrillas in the Balkans. As a result the Americans believed that he wished to divert the main Allied action to the Balkans, despite his repeated and sincere insistence that he was anxious that "Overlord" be properly prepared and carried out as soon as possible.

The conferences at Cairo and Teheran resulted in a decision on a target date for "Overlord" in May, 1944, dependent on the moon and the tides. General Eisenhower was named Supreme Commander. Command in the Mediterranean would be taken over by the British.

At Teheran, also, Stalin announced to his allies his intention to declare war on Japan after the defeat of Germany. Such action, Churchill thought, justified his views that bases in China were not important, for with Russia in the fight more useful bases for attacking Japan would become available in Siberia.

Churchill had not felt well during the conferences, and on his way back to London from Cairo he became very ill with pneumonia. His doctor, Lord Moran, put him to bed in Tunis. After he recovered, he went on to Marrakesh, in Morocco, to recuperate. Although his return to London was delayed for several weeks, he continued to follow the operations and to exert influence on the direction of the war by radio.

The Problem of Landing Craft

Churchill had always believed that control of the sea should be exploited by amphibious landings to outflank an enemy. When progress stopped in Italy he urged that such an operation be made farther up the peninsula. Eisenhower agreed and began to plan an attack from the sea near Anzio, between Cassino and Rome. There were enough landing craft available for only about one division, however, since the remainder of those in the Mediterranean were supposed to leave for England and the "Overlord" buildup during the last weeks of 1943 and the first weeks of 1944. Consequently Eisenhower's plans were at first based on a one-division landing.

The local military staffs, however, were of the opinion that at least two divisions would be required for the Anzio operation. With this Churchill agreed, even though the use of men and landing craft in such an operation would mean no hope for the operation he very much wanted against Rhodes. Yet the schedule for landing craft was so rigid that only he and the President together could change it. Roosevelt agreed to delay transferring fifty-six LST's from the Mediterranean for three weeks, provided as always that "Overlord" should remain the paramount operation, and that these craft would reach Britain in time for that.

Shortly after Churchill's return to London, Admiral Mountbatten sent his chief planner, American Major General Albert C. Wedemeyer, to present the SEAC plans for action in Southeast Asia. Mountbatten advocated building up the air route into China over "the Hump," and abandoning the plan to build

Churchill and General Dwight D. Eisenhower review United States troops
as the Allies approach the launching of the D-Day offensive. (UPI)

162

a land route through Burma. This would free troops to attack the Malay Peninsula and Sumatra as the first step of an advance east and north through the Dutch East Indies and along the coast of Asia. This program had Churchill's support; he thought it would have immediate psychological and political effects in the countries of Southeast Asia and would hasten the defeat of Japan.

Roosevelt and the American Joint Chiefs of Staff did not share the views of Churchill and Mountbatten. When Wedemeyer presented the plan in Washington he found that the land operations in Burma were considered more important; there was doubt that there would be enough landing craft and other equipment available for the amphibious attack. The appearance of the main Japanese fleet at Singapore in March, furthermore, meant the end of British naval superiority in the area, and ruled out any possibility of an amphibious operation.

Nevertheless Churchill, after ascertaining that the American planners did not require British naval support in the Pacific at least until the summer of 1945, ordered that plans be developed for an amphibious operation across the Bay of Bengal against the Malay Peninsula, with the recapture of Singapore its ultimate objective. The plan would be ready when resources became available.

CHAPTER 10

Triumph and Tragedy

Suspicion Among Allies

Plans for "Overlord" were well advanced by the time Churchill returned to England after his illness. The target date was now the first week in June, 1944. Churchill at once plunged into the study of the details of these plans, and resumed his flood of memoranda on a wide range of subjects, but mostly about the forthcoming landing on the beaches of Normandy.

Churchill planned to observe the assault at firsthand from the deck of a British warship supporting the landing on June 6. Eisenhower finally dissuaded him from this, but shortly after the landings Churchill visited the headquarters of British General Sir Bernard L. Montgomery, the land-force commander in Normandy. The Prime Minister also walked over the beaches, littered with the debris of battle. He was particularly interested in observing the unloading operations at the artificial harbor that he had conceived.

At Teheran it had been agreed that an attack with ten divisions should be made on southern France at the same time that "Overlord" was launched, to draw German troops away from

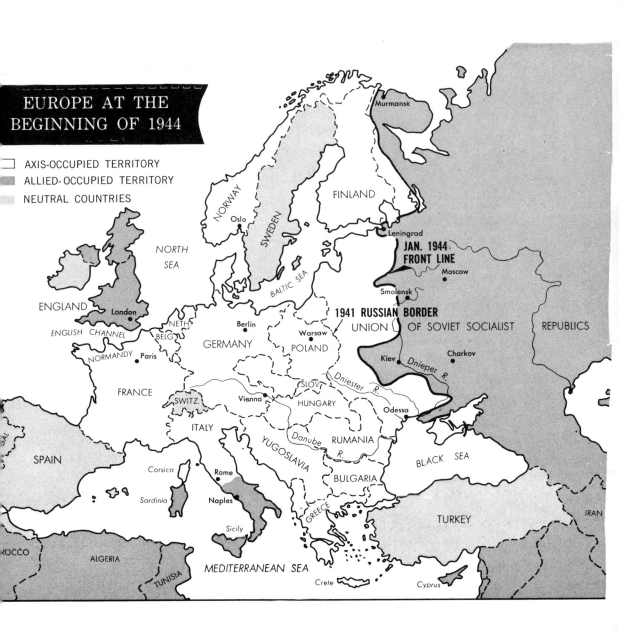

EUROPE AT THE BEGINNING OF 1944

☐ AXIS-OCCUPIED TERRITORY
▨ ALLIED-OCCUPIED TERRITORY
▨ NEUTRAL COUNTRIES

Murmansk

NORWAY

Oslo

SWEDEN

FINLAND

NORTH SEA

BALTIC SEA

Leningrad

JAN. 1944 FRONT LINE

Moscow

Smolensk

1941 RUSSIAN BORDER

ENGLAND

London

UNION OF SOVIET SOCIALIST REPUBLICS

ENGLISH CHANNEL

NETH.

Berlin

Warsaw

BELG.

GERMANY

POLAND

Kiev

Charkov

Dnieper R.

NORMANDY

Paris

SLOV.

Dniester R.

FRANCE

SWITZ.

Vienna

HUNGARY

Odessa

ITALY

YUGOSLAVIA

Danube R.

RUMANIA

SPAIN

Corsica

Rome

BULGARIA

BLACK SEA

Sardinia

Naples

GREECE

TURKEY

IRAN

Sicily

ROCCO

ALGERIA

TUNISIA

MEDITERRANEAN SEA

Crete

Cyprus

Normandy. This operation, known as "Anvil," was dependent upon the use of troops from Italy and so could not be undertaken until the main objectives in Italy—Rome, and the strategic airfields—had been secured. "Anvil's" value was originally believed to be dependent upon its being carried out simultaneously with "Overlord." When the capture of Rome was delayed, it began to seem doubtful that troops would be available for "Anvil" by June. Since the Anzio landings had drawn eight or ten German divisions away from France, in Churchill's view this had really accomplished the purpose for which "Anvil" was designed.

By the time Rome was captured, on June 4, it was apparent that "Anvil" could not be attempted until mid-August, and Churchill urged that it should be abandoned. He felt that a feint at the Riviera would have as much effect on the deployment of German troops as a real attack, and that the armies in Italy could be used more profitably elsewhere. He agreed with the British commanders in Italy and the Mediterranean, Generals Alexander and Wilson, that it would be more desirable to move up to the Po Valley and to make an amphibious landing on the Istrian Peninsula and Trieste, possibly to be followed by an advance into Austria and Hungary. Not only would this divert German divisions from the operations on the Western and Eastern Fronts, but it would put forces of the Western Allies in a strategic position in relation to Russia when hostilities ended. It was already apparent to Churchill that Soviet views on the future of Eastern Europe differed greatly from those of Britain and the United States.

The American chiefs and Roosevelt feared that a move to Istria and Trieste would be followed by a plea for armies to fight in the Balkans, although Churchill did not mention this possibility. They had never agreed with Churchill's ideas about the vulnerability of the "soft under-belly of the Axis." They now looked upon Churchill's proposal for the abandonment of "Anvil" as evidence that he was more interested in reestablishing British influence in Southeastern Europe than he was in hastening the end of the war by a direct assault against Germany.

The Americans believed that there should be only one major operation against Germany, that in northern France, and that nothing should be done that was not directly related to this. The Joint Chiefs of Staff accepted General Eisenhower's view that the quickest way to open up a new port to receive additional troops and equipment from the United States would be to carry out "Anvil" and take the port of Marseilles. The assault troops could then move up the Rhone Valley and meet the forces working east from Normandy in time to join the fight for the Ruhr. Thus the Americans saw "Anvil" as being much more than a strategic diversion to confuse and overextend the Germans; it was also a means of providing logistical support and manpower reinforcements for the main Allied effort in northern France.

It was finally decided, after much correspondence between Roosevelt and Churchill, to proceed with "Anvil," now renamed "Dragoon." In early August, however, the successful breakout from Normandy led Churchill to recommend that the ten divisions intended for "Dragoon" be sent by sea directly to

Brittany. In this way they could join Eisenhower's forces at once and put their weight into the main drive eastward toward Germany, rather than landing against defended shores in the south, next fighting west to take Toulon and Marseilles, and then fighting up the Rhone Valley. Instead of a diversion they would be part of the main operation from the beginning.

By this time, however, the Americans distrusted any suggestion from Churchill about this operation and Roosevelt remained unconvinced. Churchill yielded to the American determination to continue with "Dragoon."

The American suspicions of Churchill's motives were to some extent correct, but they misinterpreted his objectives. Until the day of the landings on the Riviera, Churchill continued to hope that "Dragoon," which to him seemed purposeless, would be abandoned and the troops used to greater advantage in northern Italy and farther to the east. But his intent was not to undermine or to reduce the effectiveness of the "Overlord" operation. On the contrary, he hoped to make it more effective by forcing a greater dispersal of German forces, and by assuring the Western Allies of a solid position in Central Europe at the end of the war.

Ultimately the operation in southern France resulted in the junction of armies from the south with those from the north and the opening of another line of communications in France. But Churchill always felt that the advantages gained at the cost of considerable casualties in southern France did not anywhere near equal the advantages that would have resulted from a strong attack into the Po Valley in northern Italy, and an advance to Vienna and the Danube Valley from the south before the Russians could reach it from the east. He did not believe that this diversion of a relatively small Allied force from northern France would delay the defeat of Germany; it might even hasten Hitler's downfall, and would certainly reduce Soviet postwar dominance in Southeastern and Central Europe.

"Communism Raised Its Head"

Churchill was by this time much concerned by Communist activity in Italy, Greece, and the Balkans. With the Russian armies approaching from the east, he realized that the Communists would probably dominate the local governments, and the Western Allies, distant as they were from the region, could do very little to prevent this. Yet for several years Britain had been supporting governments-in-exile for several of the countries occupied by Germany. She was pledged to help restore them to their capitals upon their liberation. This would be impossible if the Soviets set up Communist governments in these countries.

In May, 1944, Churchill had proposed that the Russians take responsibility for Rumania, as the military occupying power, while Britain took responsibility for Greece. Stalin was prepared to accept this suggestion. But when Churchill asked Roosevelt for his agreement to this, he found the President and his Secretary of State, Cordell Hull, unwilling to agree to anything that seemed to be setting up spheres of influence. Although Roosevelt did agree to a three-month trial of Churchill's proposed arrangement, he saw no real danger that the whole area would end up in the Communist camp. The President was convinced that Stalin was sincere in protesting any deviation from earlier Allied agreement that all liberated countries should select their own future governments.

A strong Communist movement, the EAM, had been developing in Greece. Churchill was determined that the Greek government-in-exile should be returned to Athens as soon as the Germans left or were driven from the country. He succeeded in getting Roosevelt's agreement to a plan to land some British troops in Athens as soon as opportunity offered. The Greek government would follow close behind them, leaving no time for the Communists to set up a government when the Germans withdrew.

With "Overlord" well on its way and the defeat of Germany only a matter of time and hard fighting, the British and American chiefs met again at Quebec in September, 1944, for the "Octagon" Conference. Churchill went determined to reach agreement on a full share for Britain in the war against Japan and a plan to regain her possessions in the Far East. The British fleet was by then available to be sent in strength to the Pacific, and the Royal Air Force could follow as soon as Germany was defeated. In Burma, Mountbatten needed more troops in order to carry out both land and amphibious operations to take Rangoon and ultimately Singapore.

At Quebec, Churchill secured agreement that no more troops would be removed from Italy until the results of the offensive currently under way in General Alexander's command were known. Landing craft would be left in the Mediterranean at least until October for a possible assault on Istria. Thereafter they would be needed for the amphibious attack on Rangoon, which was to be combined with a land advance into Burma from the north.

The Russian armies had moved into Rumania and Bulgaria. In Churchill's words, "Communism raised its head behind the thundering Russian battlefront. Russia was the Deliverer, and Communism the Gospel she brought. . . . Communism . . . slid on before, as well as followed, the onward march of the mighty armies directed from the Kremlin."

Churchill was anxious that communism be controlled at least in the two nations for which he felt a particular responsibility: Poland, for which Britain had entered the war, and Greece, where British soldiers had tried vainly to stem the German advance. His attempts to restore the pre-war boundaries of Poland and a government representative of the people were thwarted, however, by Soviet plans for incorporating former Polish lands into the Soviet Union and for installing a Communist government in Warsaw.

In Greece, on the other hand, as the Germans withdrew up the Peloponnese in early October, 1944, British troops landed at Patras and worked their way up the peninsula to Athens. Greek government officials landed at Piraeus on October 17. The Communist-dominated groups that had been active for some time in Greece, in spite of earlier agreements to cooperate, soon tried to seize the government and civil war followed.

At the Yalta Conference in February, 1945, Churchill, Roosevelt, and Stalin met to talk about what should be done after Germany's defeat. President Roosevelt, looking drawn and ill, would be dead in a few short weeks, thus increasing Churchill's fears concerning world peace. (UPI)

On Churchill's orders, the British troops in Greece took military action to prevent a Communist take-over, and were soon involved in the fighting. A large segment of world opinion condemned Churchill's action, but he stood steadfastly by his decision, in the belief that communism was a very real threat to the future peace of the world. Within the next few years many of his strongest critics had accepted his views.

The Defeat of Germany

By the beginning of 1945 it was certain that Hitler could not hold out much longer against the onrushing armies approaching Germany from west and east. In February, Churchill, Roosevelt, and Stalin met at Yalta, in the Crimea, to discuss what should be done after the collapse of Germany. The greater part of their discussion was concerned with political or diplomatic questions. The most important military decision was how Stalin would carry out his agreement to enter the war against Japan after Hitler's defeat. The British were not consulted on American-Russian negotiations to accomplish this; Churchill's only contribution was to sign the agreement after it had been completed. Churchill was alarmed by Roosevelt's obvious determination to improve relations with Stalin, even at the expense of the Anglo-American alliance. He was also concerned by evidence of Roosevelt's declining health.

The last months of the war against Germany were full of frustrations for Churchill. He was convinced that Russia's policies and actions were a serious threat to the peace of the world and that steps must be taken to gain for the Western Allies the most advantageous position possible from which to face the problems of the postwar years. Attempts to secure a popularly supported, representative government in Poland were thwarted by Soviet disregard for the recommendations and pleadings of Churchill and Roosevelt. There, as in Bulgaria and Rumania, the invading Russians placed Communists in control of the government.

Russia must be stopped, Churchill thought, and it was essential that British and American armies advance as far east as possible, and particularly into Berlin and Prague. He was convinced of the political and psychological importance of occupying these two cities rather than permitting the Russians to do so. But Roosevelt still did not visualize the Soviet threat as Churchill did.

With American General Eisenhower the Supreme Commander in Europe, and three-fourths of the armies he commanded American, Churchill alone could make no strategic decisions. He was unable to convince Eisenhower or Marshall or the failing Roosevelt that postwar political advantages should be a determining factor in the development of military strategy for the final defeat of Germany. Churchill alone could not hope to check the Soviet determination to control as much European territory as possible. The movements of the Allied armies were not his to direct.

Roosevelt's death on April 12, 1945, increased Churchill's pessimism about the future, for he felt that action must be taken quickly to hold the Communists. President Truman was inexperienced and uninformed; it was unlikely that he could be persuaded promptly of the vital importance of the problem. At the time when the greatest decisions about the postwar world must be taken, an unknown and unsure hand was in command in the United States.

The official surrender of Germany took place on May 8, 1945. In a telegram to President Truman four days later Churchill recommended that they must "come to an understanding with Russia, or see where we are with her, before we weaken our armies mortally or retire to the zones of occupation." Already the American armies were being removed from Europe and sent to the Pacific. As for what the Russian armies were doing, "An iron curtain is drawn down upon their front," said Churchill. "We do not know what is going on behind."

Defeat at the Polls

As the war moved toward a close, Churchill realized that Britain's coalition government, which had worked together so well when the main efforts of the government were channeled toward military victory, could not be continued after hostilities ended. Under the British system he must submit to the king his resignation as Prime Minister and call for election of a new Parliament. In May, 1945, he resigned and was renamed Prime Minister. He then appointed ministers and other officials from his own, Conservative, party. Elections were set for July 5. The results, in order to allow time for receipt of ballots from troops overseas, would be counted three weeks later.

On July 15, Churchill, Truman, and Stalin and their staffs met for the last major war conference in Potsdam, Germany, to discuss some of the crucial problems of boundaries, peace settlements, and the numerous other matters which could best be settled at the top level. On July 25 Churchill flew home to await the election results. He did not return to Potsdam, for the Conservatives lost their majority in Parliament, and he was no longer Prime Minister.

On July 26 Churchill gave his resignation to the king, in order that the new Prime Minister, Clement Attlee, could complete the conversations at Potsdam with full power.

An Assessment

Certainly the British people had not rejected Churchill because of any failure as a director of war. The electoral defeat was the result of internal conditions in Britain, which Churchill had ignored, and which he perhaps did not fully understand; conditions which became increasingly more important to the British people as peace gradually returned to their embattled island.

It is possible that the British people, even today, do not fully realize the brilliance of the strategic genius that had guided them to victory. No man since Napoleon had so completely and so thoroughly controlled and guided far-flung forces in combat; and Napoleon never had to cope with global warfare. Hitler's direction of Germany's war effort was unquestionably more dictatorial, but it is doubtful if Hitler kept himself as fully informed of all aspects of the war as did Churchill, and certainly the German dictator lacked the British Prime Minister's uncanny prescience and practical wisdom.

No reader of Churchill's writings on the two world wars can avoid amazement at the soundness and correctness of Churchill's assessments and forecasts. His critics can accuse him of stacking evidence in his memoirs to support his version of past controversies, but no such criticism is possible when judgments and forecasts are confirmed months and years after a speech was delivered or a book published.

A few examples will suffice: his assessment of Pétain, based upon World War I observation, and substantiated in 1940; his favorable assessment of Greek troops despite their defeat by the Turks in 1923, substantiated by their 1940 victories over the Italians; his recognition of the capabilities of Turkish leader Mustafa Kemal, even though he was an enemy; his understanding of the nature of Nazism, and of Hitler's objectives, when all of the peace-loving world refused to believe; his similar assessment of communism and Communist objectives before, during, and after World War II; his understanding of the significance of the buildup of German air power in the mid-1930's; his recognition of the basic concept of deterrence—even though the term had not yet been given its current strategic significance—in the years before and since World War II.

That was the kind of thinking which this great man applied to strategic problems around the world throughout the war and which—as proven by hindsight—was more realistic, more imaginative, and more effective than that of most Americans and of most of Churchill's British subordinates.

The impact of the tremendous mass of ideas and schemes spewed forth from Churchill's energetic and imaginative intellect was a severe trial for his subordinates and created great problems for them. He was feared and mistrusted—as well as admired and respected—by the military staffs of his American allies. We have ample evidence from memoirs that his minutes and memoranda were the despair of his own Chiefs of Staff Committee and its planning and administrative staffs. His principal military adviser, Field Marshal Lord Brooke, Chief of the Imperial General Staff, complained more about the time and effort expended in trying to dissuade Churchill from imaginative but unrealistic schemes than he did about any of the hardships of war at the front or in tedious headquarters work. Brooke and the other chiefs of staff were constantly frustrated by Churchill's meddling. Yet they were stimulated and inspired by his brilliant and imaginative suggestions.

Unquestionably many of Churchill's ideas were unrealistic, and he was as quick to recognize their shortcomings as anyone else. In fact he used his personal staff and the Chiefs of Staff Committee at least in part as a sounding board. While he was often reluctant to abandon ideas that were sometimes more romantic than realistic, it is important to note that he never overrode the unanimous professional advice of his military advisers, even when he was in disagreement. This is only one of the many respects in which Churchill's genius as a war leader was so much greater than that of his rival, Hitler.

In retrospect there can be no doubt that Churchill's belief that military strategy should serve political policy was far wiser than the more single-minded, militarily dominant strategy of the Americans. There are differences of opinion among professional and amateur strategists studying World War II as to the difficulties that the Allies would have encountered had they diverted some of their military strength from northwest to southeast Europe, and as to the effect this would have had upon Germany's ability to continue resistance. In retrospect, however, it is clear that many problems of the cold war would have been avoided had such operations been conducted at the time and in the manner Churchill wanted, regardless of the cost in effort and time. And regardless of the scale of effort that this would have required, it is hard to see how the cost in resources of material or manpower could have been greater, or how it could have delayed the ultimate collapse of Germany.

Churchill has also been criticized for the emphasis that he put on the strategic air bombardment of Germany. It has been suggested that the resources squandered in the so-called "Passchendaele of the air" would have been better employed in the construction of more landing craft and in the buildup of amphibious ground forces to employ these craft. Such an argument overlooks many of the factors which caused Churchill to lend his support to the Combined Bomber Offensive.

In the first place, when this air bombardment assault of Germany began, this was the only important way that Britain had to strike back against Germany, and to give really effective support to the Russian ally. Prior to 1944 no other use of this manpower and munitions production effort could have paid greater dividends. Heavy though the losses of Bomber Command were during these years, it is hard to see how this skilled and expensive combat manpower could have been employed elsewhere without far greater loss of life. It is doubtful that a reduction of the bombing effort against Germany in 1944 and 1945, with a comparable increase in the scale of ground combat operations, could have hastened the end of the war, or reduced British sacrifice of manpower. In fact, one is almost bound to draw a completely opposite conclusion.

Bearing all of these things in mind, the conclusion still seems clear. Churchill knew, understood, and controlled his nation's war effort with a skill and surety unseen since the time of Napoleon.

CHAPTER 11

Writing About Wars, and Other Things

Thoughts on Past, Present, and Future

Churchill was badly hurt when the British people rejected him in the 1945 election, after he had pulled them through the dark days of the war and given them victory over Hitler, and near victory in Japan. Overnight he had changed from the most influential man in his nation and one of the most important and knowledgeable men in the world, to one with no major responsibilities and few demands on his time.

After six years of war, however, Churchill was physically worn out. The enforced rest was probably good for him. He had passed his seventieth birthday the preceding November. He had been charging from one thing to another, working late into the night, and sleeping little while he carried the immense burdens of the almost unlimited powers he had assumed in 1940. For several months after his electoral defeat, he relaxed completely, finding the diversion he needed in long hours of painting. Slowly he built up his strength and made his adjustment to a new mode of life.

Churchill at first turned down or set aside pleas that he should write his account of World War II. In time, however, he yielded and went to work on the six volumes of *The Second World War*, based on his own contemporary records as well as his memory. For enjoyable reading as well as for source material for future historians the books have no equal. Even before this work was completed he returned to labors on a book he had started many years before, *History of the English-Speaking Peoples*.

Churchill received many invitations and honors, and people listened to what he had to say, even though he had no position in the British government. During a visit to the United States in March, 1946, he spoke at Westminster College in Fulton, Missouri. His speech, which he called "The Sinew of Peace," has come to be called "The Iron Curtain Speech," for in it he used publicly for the first time the phrase he had earlier used in his message to President Truman in May, 1945, to describe the division between west and east in Europe. On this occasion and on many others he called for "the fraternal association of the English-speaking peoples . . . a special relationship between the British Commonwealth and Empire and the United States."

He described the threat of communism on this side of the iron curtain and expressed his view that war was not inevitable, but that a firm settlement should be reached with Russia, under the United Nations.

If the population of the English-speaking Commonwealths be added to that of the United States with all that such cooperation implies in the air, on the sea, all over the globe and in science and in industry, and in moral force, there will be no quivering, precarious balance of power to offer its temptation to ambition or adventure. On the contrary, there will be an overwhelming assurance of security. If we adhere faithfully to the Charter of the United Nations and walk forward in sedate and sober strength seeking no one's land or treasure, seeking to lay no arbitrary control upon the thoughts of men; if all British moral and material forces and convictions are joined with your own in fraternal association, the highroads of the future will be clear, not only for us but for all, not only for our time, but for a century to come.

Churchill's solution was not tried in the complete and thorough union he desired. But his clear statements of the threat to world peace caused men to think, and certainly contributed to the hardening of the United States position against Communist aggression, and to the creation of the North Atlantic Treaty Organization.

Churchill remained on the sidelines for about a year before he again took an active part in politics as Leader of the Opposition. In the House of Commons, with his old fighting spirit, he began to lead attacks on the Labour government and its policies.

In October, 1951, a general election in England returned the Conservative party to power. Churchill, as party leader, once more became Prime Minister. It was different, however, for there was no war to unify the nation. The problems of England were to a great extent domestic, and Churchill had never been attuned to the problems of the common man of Britain. Nor did he really understand the critically important financial situation. Moreover, the years were telling on him. He had had a slight stroke, and his pace had slowed down. His mind was still alert, but no longer did he send forth a steady stream of ideas, or concern himself with all details of important matters.

Slowed down though he was, however, Churchill fought valiantly to survive, both physically and politically. A second and more serious stroke in 1953 seemed to many of his family and friends to mean the end of his political career. But Churchill rallied and continued to carry on from crisis to crisis of world affairs. No longer able to give the job of Prime Minister the full time and attention it needed, he still so hated the thought of retirement that he set the date further and further into the future. He seemed to believe—with some reason—that even with his powers impaired he was more capable than any of his subordinates. When he finally left the office, on April 6, 1955, it was at the request of the party and not of his own decision.

A few months earlier, on his eightieth birthday, November 30, 1954, Churchill had made a speech that was his real farewell to the nation:

Sir Winston Churchill at eighty-five. He is shown here riding from Washington's National Airport with President Eisenhower on a visit to the United States in 1959. (UPI)

I have never accepted what many people have kindly said—namely that I inspired the nation. Their will was resolute and remorseless, and as it proved unconquerable. It fell to me to express it, and if I found the right words you must remember that I have always earned my living by my pen and by my tongue. It was the nation and the race dwelling all round the globe that had the lion's heart. I had the luck to be called upon to give the roar.

He lived for ten more years, gradually fading in all his faculties, a sad and lingering end to an incomparable life.

185

Chronology

1874, November 30	Birth of Winston Churchill
1894	Graduation from Sandhurst as army subaltern
1895	Observing guerrilla warfare in Cuba
1896–98	Military service in India
1898	Publication of *The Malakand Field Force*
1898, September 1	Battle of Omdurman
1899	Churchill resigns from the army
1899, July	Defeated in Parliamentary election in Oldham
1899–1900	War correspondent in South African war
1899, December	Escape from Boer prison camp
1901, January	Elected to Parliament from Oldham
1906–8	Undersecretary of State for the Colonies

1908–10	President of the Board of Trade; first Cabinet position
1910–11	Home Secretary
1911–15	First Lord of the Admiralty
1914, July	Test mobilization of the British fleet
1914, July 28	Outbreak of World War I
1914, October 3–7	Battle of Antwerp
1914, Oct.–Dec.	Churchill proposes "land cruisers," prototypes of tanks
1915, March 18	Allied fleet repulsed at the Dardanelles
1915, April 25	Allied land assault on Gallipoli Peninsula
1915, May 26	Churchill dismissed from the Admiralty
1915–16, Nov.–July	Military service in France
1917–18	Minister of Munitions
1918, November	Armistice ends World War I
1919–21	Secretary of State for War and for Air
1921–22	Secretary of State for the Colonies
1922, November	Defeated in Parliamentary election
1923–31	Publication of *The World Crisis*
1924, September	Reelected to Parliament from Epping

1924–29	Chancellor of the Exchequer in Baldwin government
1929–39	Member of Parliament outside the government
1932–39	Warnings about Germany
1938, September 29	The Munich Conference
1939, September 1	Outbreak of World War II
1939, September 3	Britain declares war; Churchill First Lord of the Admiralty
1940, April–May	Struggle for Norway
1940, May 10	German assault in the West; Churchill Prime Minister
1940, May 26–June 3	Evacuation from Dunkirk
1940, June 10	Italy declares war against Britain and France
1940, June 25	Surrender of France
1940, July 10–Oct. 31	Battle of Britain
1940, October 28	Italian invasion of Greece
1940–41, Dec.–Feb.	Wavell's first desert offensive
1941, March–May	Rommel's first desert offensive
1941, April 6–29	German conquest of Yugoslavia and Greece
1941, May 20–June 1	Battle of Crete
1941, May–July	Campaigns in Iraq and Syria
1941, June 22	German invasion of Russia

1941, August 9–12	Atlantic Conference, Placentia Bay, Newfoundland
1941, Nov.–Dec.	Auchinleck's Offensive in Cyrenaica
1941, December 7–8	Outbreak of war with Japan
1941–42, Dec.–Jan.	"Arcadia" Conference, Washington, D.C.
1942, Jan.–June	Rommel's second desert offensive
1942, February 15	Surrender of Singapore
1942, June 18–21	Washington Conference
1942, Oct. 23–Nov. 4	Battle of El Alamein
1942, November 8	Allied landings in North Africa, operation "Torch"
1943, Jan. 14–23	Casablanca Conference
1943, May 12–25	"Trident" Conference, Washington, D.C.
1943, May 13	Allies complete conquest of Tunisia
1943, July–Aug.	Allied conquest of Sicily
1943, August 14–24	"Quadrant" Conference, Quebec
1943, September 8	Surrender of Italy
1943, Nov.–Dec.	"Sextant" Conference, Cairo
1943, Nov. 28–30	"Eureka" Conference, Teheran
1944, January 22	Allied landings at Anzio
1944, June 4	Fall of Rome

1944, June 6	Allied landings in Normandy, Operation "Overlord"
1944, Aug. 14	Allied landings on French Riviera, Operation "Anvil"– "Dragoon"
1944, September 12–16	"Octagon" Conference, Quebec
1945, February 4–9	"Magneto" Conference, Yalta
1945, April 12	Death of Roosevelt
1945, May 8	Surrender of Germany
1945, July 16–Aug. 2	"Terminal" Conference, Potsdam
1945, July 26	Churchill government defeated in national elections
1951–55, Oct.–Apr.	Churchill Prime Minister
1965, Jan. 24	Death of Sir Winston Churchill

Appendix

Principles of Military Leadership and Military Theory

Since different people have different ideas about leadership and about how it is defined and recognized, a few paragraphs are necessary to explain how the word "leadership" is applied in this book to the military career of one of the outstanding men of history.

Military Leadership

In its simplest terms, *leadership* means the ability of a person to influence and direct other people to work cooperatively together toward a goal or objective, because that individual commands their obedience, confidence, and respect. But these words are really meaningful only if we can relate them to observable standards of performance. One set of standards to show the qualities of a military leader is the following:

*Professional military skill or competence.** This includes a knowledge and understanding of past military events (or military history), an understanding of theoretical principles of warfare, and a combination of judgment and energy in applying this knowledge and theory to a variety of different situations.

* Churchill is probably the only example in history of an essentially civilian leader of a nation at war who was truly professional in tactics and techniques of warfare as well as in broad matters of strategy.

Understanding of the human tools of the leader. This simply means that a leader must know the capabilities and limitations of his men.

Insistence upon high standards of training and discipline. In this way the leader, knowing his men, is able to make the most of their capabilities and to eliminate or reduce their weaknesses and limitations.

Inspirational ability. The leader must be able to project his personality to his men, so that they recognize the quality of his leadership and respond to it with confidence.

Personal courage. The leader must be able to set an example for his men. But in addition to willingness to face the dangers and risks of battle, he must have moral courage off the battlefield to make difficult decisions which lesser men might try to avoid.

Perseverance and determination in adversity. Some men can perform well when everything seems to be going their way. One important measure of human greatness is a person's ability to keep on striving for success, even when his best plans and actions seem to be resulting in failure.

The ability, in peace and war, to understand the relationship between military strategy and national policy. This is as true of a king-general, like Alexander the Great, or a civilian director of war, like Winston Churchill, as it is of the general who is controlled by civilian authority, like George Washington.

These are the seven standards, or yardsticks, of leadership which provide a basis for selecting the great captains. All of these standards are simple, and easy to understand, although their relationship together is so difficult that only a handful of men have been able to measure up close to the maximum of all of these standards.

The reader who is not intimately acquainted with military theory may find some problems with the first of the above standards, in recognizing the ability of a leader to apply military theory and principles to different situations. All that we really need to know, however, to understand the professional military qualities of military leadership which made the great captains great, is the nature of the principles of war and the relationship between strategy and tactics.

Military Theory

Over the past century, military theorists have formulated lists of *Principles of War* which are believed to include all of the fundamental elements of success in waging war. There are some differences among the lists prepared by different theorists, but since they are all based upon review and analysis of historical examples, these various lists are generally consistent with each other. There are differences of opinion as to the applicability of these principles to warfare in the future, but there is no doubt that they provide a useful measurement for past conflicts, since they are derived from, and based upon, the experience of the past.

In this series we use the following list of nine principles of war:

Objective. Every military operation should be directed to accomplish a decisive, realistic objective. The ultimate objective of any conflict is to destroy the enemy's capability and desire to continue the conflict. Intermediate objectives should contribute directly to attaining this ultimate objective. Objectives should be selected after due consideration of the characteristics of the area of conflict, and the resources and military forces which both sides can employ in the conflict.

Offensive. Only offensive action can achieve decisive results, since only by attacking or advancing can a military leader accomplish his objective by forcing his will on the enemy. Sometimes circumstances are such that a commander must take defensive action because the enemy is stronger, or in a more favorable position. But a leader on the defensive should always be seeking to find an opportunity where he can seize the initiative and press toward the achievement of his objective by offensive action. Other principles of war can help him in this search.

Simplicity. A commander must plan his operations and organize his forces so that they are as simple and uncomplicated as possible. When hundreds or thousands of men must work together to accomplish a plan, even the most simple plan may fail. The possibility for confusion and failure is even greater when men and commanders are frightened and excited in the course of a battle.

Control. (This is sometimes called "Unity of Command" or "Cooperation.") There must be one controlling authority to assure the decisive employment of all men and forces toward the achievement of an objective. This controlling authority achieves unity of effort by coordinating the actions of all forces available to him and assures cooperation between all of the individual people or forces engaged in the conflict.

Mass. (This is sometimes called "Concentration.") The maximum available combat power should be applied at the point and at the time which will best assure a decisive success. By seizing the initiative and concentrating forces rapidly and efficiently, a smaller force can often apply greater combat power at the decisive point than a larger enemy force. Mass is not dependent upon numbers alone but results from a combination of manpower, firepower, and fighting capability. Superior weapons, tactics, and morale can contribute to the effectiveness of mass.

Economy of Forces. (This is sometimes called "Economy of Effort.") A commander should employ only the absolute minimum of forces or resources at points which are not decisive. This will permit him to accomplish the principles of the objective and of mass at decisive times and places. Defensive action, or deception, at the less important points will help a commander achieve economy of forces.

Maneuver. Maneuver is the positioning, or the moving, of forces in such a way as to place the enemy at a relative disadvantage. By maneuver a commander can apply the principles of mass and the offensive at a decisive point where the enemy is not adequately prepared or positioned to meet an attack.

Surprise. This is accomplished by striking an enemy at a time, or in a place, or in a manner, that he does not expect. Surprise is particularly important for the commander of a force which does not otherwise have combat superiority to the enemy. Surprise can be achieved by speed, secrecy, deception, variations in fighting methods, and by moving through regions

196

which the enemy does not think are passable for military forces.

Security. This means that a commander must take those measures which will prevent the enemy from surprising him, or from interfering with his operations. With adequate security, a commander can then apply the other principles of war, and employ his own forces in the most effective manner possible.

These principles of war are obviously very general in their nature; they apply to large forces and to small, and to extensive campaigns as well as to brief engagements. Military men usually say that they are applicable to both tactical and strategic operations. This means that the nonmilitary reader should have a clear understanding of the difference between strategy and tactics.

Many, many thousands of words have been written to describe strategy and tactics, and to explain the difference between the two terms. But really the distinction is not difficult.

Military strategy is the art of employing all of the resources available to a military commander for the purpose of achieving a successful outcome in a conflict against hostile armed forces.

Military tactics is the technique of assembling, positioning, and moving some specific portion of the forces available to a commander in order to contribute to the accomplishment of the goals or objectives of strategy.

In other words, strategy concerns the employment and disposition of all means of forces within a commander's power in order to achieve the desired result of a war or campaign. Tactics concerns the specific battlefield methods of employment of these means or forces.

Table 1

COMPARATIVE NAVAL STRENGTHS, 1914

	British			German		
	Total	Home Waters	Grand Fleet[1]	Total	Home Waters	High Seas Fleet
Dreadnoughts[2] (modern battleships)	20	(20)	(20)	13	(13)	(13)
Battle Cruisers[3]	8	(4)	(4)	5	(4)	(4)
Old Battleships[2]	40	(38)	(10)	22	(22)	(10)
Cruisers[4]	102	(48)	(21)	41	(32)	(17)
Destroyers	301	(270)	(50)	144	(144)	(80)
Submarines	78	(65)	(9)	30	(30)	(24)[5]

[1] Numbers of cruisers and destroyers in the Grand Fleet are approximate, and varied considerably during early days of war.

[2] Dreadnoughts were modern, big-gun ships, completely outclassing all old battleships (see discussion in text). Britain had two more dreadnoughts completed, but not yet ready for action, and fifteen under construction (including three that had been intended for other nations). Germany had three more completed, but not yet ready for action, and four under construction.

[3] Vessels carrying heavy guns similar to dreadnoughts, but with thinner armor and greater speed. Britain and Germany each had one additional battle cruiser completed but not yet ready for action. Britain had one building; Germany had two building.

[4] Included old armored cruisers and smaller, but faster and better armed, light cruisers.

[5] Records are conflicting on exact number of German submarines in commission. This figure is approximately correct.

Table 2

COMPARATIVE NAVAL STRENGTHS, 1939[1]

	Britain	France	Germany[2]	Italy
Battleships and Battle Cruisers[3]	18	11	4	6
"Pocket" Battleships[4]	–	–	3	–
Aircraft Carriers	10	1	1	–
Heavy Cruisers (8″ guns or more)	15	18	4	7
Light Cruisers (6″ guns or less)	62	32	6	15
Destroyers	205	34	25	59
Destroyer Escorts, Torpedo Boats, etc.	73	30	42	69
Motor Torpedo Boats	39	9	17	69
Submarines	70	72	98	115

[1] Includes ships built or nearing completion.

[2] All German vessels were newly built, and with few exceptions were more modern, faster, bigger, and generally more powerful than comparable types of other nations.

[3] Battle cruisers were as big as battleships and carried the same kind of heavy guns (usually 14″ to 16″ in caliber). But they carried less armor protection, and usually fewer heavy guns, so that, being lighter in weight, they could go faster than battleships. Thus they could hit as hard as battleships, but could not take as much punishment; they sacrificed protection for speed.

[4] Under the provisions of the Versailles Treaty after World War I, Germany was forbidden to build ships larger than 10,000 tons. The pocket battleships were really small battle cruisers; they carried 11″ guns, were very fast, but did not have much armor, so that they would not exceed the weight limit. They could beat any cruiser in the world, but could not stand up to a real battleship.

Index

204